MARIAN ANDERSON

MARIAN ANDERSON

ANNE TEDARDS

CHELSEA HOUSE PUBLISHERS

NEW YORK • PHILADELPHIA

EDITOR-IN-CHIEF: Nancy Toff
EXECUTIVE EDITOR: Remmel T. Nunn
MANAGING EDITOR: Karyn Gullen Browne
COPY CHIEF: Juliann Barbato
PICTURE EDITOR: Adrian G. Allen
ART DIRECTOR: Giannella Garrett
MANUFACTURING MANAGER: Gerald Levine

Staff for MARIAN ANDERSON:

SENIOR EDITOR: Elisa Petrini
TEXT EDITOR: Marian W. Taylor
EDITORIAL ASSISTANT: Theodore Keyes
COPYEDITOR: Michael Goodman
PICTURE RESEARCHER: Emily Miller
DESIGNER: Design Oasis
PRODUCTION COORDINATOR: Joseph Romano
COVER ILLUSTRATION: Peter Fiore

CREATIVE DIRECTOR: Harold Steinberg

3   5   7   9   8   6   4

Library of Congress Cataloging in Publication Data

Tedards, Anne. MARIAN ANDERSON

(American women of achievement)
Bibliography: p.
Includes index.
1. Anderson, Marian, 1902–   —Juvenile literature. 2. Singers—
United States—Biography—Juvenile literature. [1. Anderson,
Marian, 1902–   . 2. Singers.   3. Afro-Americans—
Biography]   I. Title. II. Series.
ML3930.A5T4   1987   782.1'092'4   [B] [92]   87-6655

ISBN 1-55546-638-9
    0-7910-0216-0 (pbk.)

CONTENTS

AMERICAN WOMEN of ACHIEVEMENT

Abigail Adams
women's rights activist

Jane Addams
social worker

Louisa May Alcott
author

Marian Anderson
singer

Susan B. Anthony
women's suffragist

Ethel Barrymore
actress

Clara Barton
*founder of the American
Red Cross*

Elizabeth Blackwell
physician

Nellie Bly
journalist

Margaret Bourke-White
photographer

Pearl Buck
author

Rachel Carson
biologist and author

Mary Cassatt
artist

Agnes De Mille
choreographer

Emily Dickinson
poet

Isadora Duncan
dancer

Amelia Earhart
aviator

Mary Baker Eddy
*founder of the Christian
Science Church*

Betty Friedan
feminist

Althea Gibson
tennis champion

Emma Goldman
revolutionary

Helen Hayes
actress

Lillian Hellman
playwright

Katherine Hepburn
actress

Karen Horney
psychoanalyst

Anne Hutchinson
religious leader

Mahalia Jackson
gospel singer

Helen Keller
humanitarian

Jeane Kirkpatrick
diplomat

Emma Lazarus
poet

Clare Boothe Luce
author and diplomat

Barbara McClintock
biologist

Margaret Mead
anthropologist

Edna St. Vincent Millay
poet

Julia Morgan
architect

Grandma Moses
painter

Louise Nevelson
sculptor

Sandra Day O'Connor
Supreme Court Justice

Georgia O'Keeffe
painter

Eleanor Roosevelt
diplomat and humanitarian

Wilma Rudolph
champion athlete

Florence Sabin
physician

Beverly Sills
singer

Gertrude Stein
author

Gloria Steinem
feminist

Harriet Beecher Stowe
author and abolitionist

Mae West
entertainer

Edith Wharton
author

Phillis Wheatley
poet

Babe Zaharias
champion athlete

CHELSEA HOUSE PUBLISHERS

"Remember the Ladies"

MATINA S. HORNER

Remember the Ladies." That is what Abigail Adams wrote to her husband John, then a delegate to the Continental Congress, as the Founding Fathers met in Philadelphia to form a new nation in March of 1776. "Be more generous and favorable to them than your ancestors. Do not put such unlimited power in the hands of the Husbands. If particular care and attention is not paid to the Ladies," Abigail Adams warned, "we are determined to foment a Rebellion, and will not hold ourselves bound by any Laws in which we have no voice, or Representation."

The words of Abigail Adams, one of the earliest American advocates of women's rights, were prophetic. Because when we have not "remembered the ladies," they have, by their words and deeds, reminded us so forcefully of the omission that we cannot fail to remember them. For the history of American women is as interesting and varied as the history of our nation as a whole. American women have played an integral part in founding, settling, and building our country. Some we remember as remarkable women who— against great odds—achieved distinction in the public arena: Anne Hutchinson, who in the 17th century became a charismatic religious leader; Phillis Wheatley, an 18th-century black slave who became a poet; Susan B. Anthony, whose name is synonymous with the 19th-century women's rights movement, and who led the struggle to enfranchise women; and, in our own century, Amelia Earhart, the first woman to cross the Atlantic Ocean by air.

These extraordinary women certainly merit our admiration, but other women, "common women," many of them all but forgotten, should also be recognized for their contributions to American thought and culture. Women have been community builders; they have founded schools and formed voluntary associations to help those in need; they have assumed the major responsibility for rearing children, passing on from one generation to the next the values that keep a culture alive. These and innumerable other contributions, once ignored, are now being recognized by scholars, students, and the public. It is exciting and gratifying to realize that a part of our history that was hardly acknowledged a few generations ago is now being studied and brought to light.

In recent decades, the field of women's history has grown from obscurity to a politically controversial splinter movement to academic respectability, in many cases mainstreamed into such traditional disciplines as history, economics, and psychology. Scholars of women, both female and male, have organized research centers at such prestigious institutions as Wellesley College, Stanford University, and the University of California. Other notable centers for women's studies are the Center for the American Woman and Politics at the Eagleton Institute of Politics at Rutgers University, the Henry A. Murray Research Center for the Study of Lives, at Radcliffe College, and the Women's Research and Education Institute, the research arm of the Congressional Caucus on Women's Issues. Other scholars and public figures have established archives and libraries, such as the Schlesinger Library on the History of Women in America, at Radcliffe College, and the Sophia Smith Collection, at Smith College, to collect and preserve the written and tangible legacies of women.

From the initial donation of the Women's Rights Collection in 1943, the Schlesinger Library grew to encompass vast collections documenting the manifold accomplishments of American women. Simultaneously, the women's movement in general and the academic discipline of women's studies in particular also began with a narrow definition and gradually expanded their mandate. Early causes such as woman suffrage and social reform, abolition and organized labor were joined by newer concerns such as the history of women in business and the professions and in politics and government; the study of the family; and social issues such as health policy and education.

Women, as historian Arthur M. Schlesinger, jr., once pointed out, "have constituted the most spectacular casualty of traditional history. They have made up at least half the human race, but you could never tell that by looking at the books historians write." The new breed of historians is remedying that omission. They have written books about immigrant women and about work-ing-class women who struggled for survival in cities and about black women who met the challenges of life in rural areas. They are telling the stories of women who, despite the barriers of tradition and economics, became lawyers and doctors and public figures.

The women's studies movement has also led scholars to question tradi-tional interpretations of their respective disciplines. For example, the study of war has traditionally been an exercise in military and political analysis, an examination of strategies planned and executed by men. But scholars of women's history have pointed out that wars have also been periods of tre-mendous change and even opportunity for women, because the very absence of men on the home front enabled them to expand their educational, eco-nomic, and professional activities and to assume leadership in their homes.

The early scholars of women's history showed a unique brand of courage in choosing to investigate new subjects and take new approaches to old ones. Often, like their subjects, they endured criticism and even ostracism by their academic colleagues. But their efforts have unquestionably been worthwhile, because with the publication of each new study and book another piece of the historical patchwork is sewn into place, revealing an increasingly com-prehensive picture of the role of women in our rich and varied history.

Such books on groups of women are essential, but books that focus on the lives of individuals are equally indispensable. Biographies can be inspirational, offering their readers the example of people with vision who have looked outside themselves for their goals and have often struggled against great obstacles to achieve them. Marian Anderson, for instance, had to overcome racial bigotry in order to perfect her art and perform as a concert singer. Isadora Duncan defied the rules of classical dance to find true artistic free-dom. Jane Addams had to break down society's notions of the proper role for women in order to create new social institutions, notably the settlement house. All of these women had to come to terms both with themselves and with the world in which they lived. Only then could they move ahead as pioneers in their chosen callings.

Biography can inspire not only by adulation but also by realism. It helps us to see not only the qualities in others that we hope to emulate, but also, perhaps, the weaknesses that made them "human." By helping us identify with the subject on a more personal level they help us to feel that we, too, can achieve such goals. We read about Eleanor Roosevelt, for instance, who occupied a unique and seemingly enviable position as the wife of the pres-ident. Yet we can sympathize with her inner dilemma: an inherently shy woman, she had to force herself to live a most public life in order to use her position to benefit others. We may not be able to imagine ourselves having the immense poetic talent of Emily Dickinson, but from her story we can understand the challenges faced by a creative woman who was expected to fulfill many family responsibilities. And though few of us will ever reach the level of athletic accomplishment displayed by Wilma Rudolph or Babe Zaharias, we can still appreciate their spirit, their overwhelming will to excel.

A biography is a multifaceted lens. It is first of all a magnification, the intimate examination of one particular life. But at the same time, it is a wide-angle lens, informing us about the world in which the subject lived. We come away from reading about one life knowing more about the social, political, and economic fabric of the time. It is for this reason, perhaps, that the great New England essayist Ralph Waldo Emerson wrote, in 1841, "There is properly no history: only biography." And it is also why biography, and particularly women's biography, will continue to fascinate writers and readers alike.

MARIAN ANDERSON

Gifted with a uniquely beautiful voice, Marian Anderson grew up with one dream: to sing on the concert stage. When she tried to enroll in music school, however, she was abruptly rejected.

ONE

Beginnings

One hot summer day in 1917, a teenager rode the streetcar to the center of Philadelphia, where she hoped to enroll in a small music school. A popular vocalist with local church groups since she was six years old, she had often been urged to try performing professionally. She knew that with formal training, she could get singing jobs to help support her widowed mother and two younger sisters.

The eager teenager had painstakingly scraped together quarters and dimes toward the music-school tuition, and her church had taken up a special collection to raise the balance. She knew she had an exceptional voice, and she firmly believed that God expected her to use this gift to its fullest potential. If developing her voice meant she could relieve her mother of her exhausting and menial work, God would surely be pleased.

She got in line with the other prospective students, all of them waiting for application blanks. But when she reached the head of the line, the receptionist looked right past her and handed a form to the applicant behind her. Then, one by one, all the others— even those who had arrived later— were given applications and told how to fill them out. At last, she was alone in the waiting room.

The receptionist eyed her coldly. "What do *you* want?" she asked.

The young woman replied timidly that she had come to inquire about entering the school.

"We don't take colored," said the receptionist, turning her back on the stunned black teenager.

Until now, the young woman had rarely encountered such prejudice; in the racially integrated neighborhood where she lived, being "colored"—a

Appointed by President Dwight Eisenhower to represent the United States at the United Nations, Marian Anderson (center front) addresses a General Assembly session in 1958.

word once routinely used to describe black people—had been no handicap. From this point on, however, she would have much experience with people who disliked—even hated—people with dark skin. Never defeated by such hostility, she would rise above it. One day, in fact, people of all races would regard her as one of the outstanding American artists of the 20th century.

Her name was Marian Anderson, and one day her deep, rich contralto voice would be heard in concert halls all over the world. She would represent her country at the United Nations, becoming a symbol of international

friendship. Anderson would be honored by presidents and queens, among other music lovers, but she would always say her proudest achievement had nothing to do with the world's recognition. "The happiest day in my life," she said, "was when I told my mother she didn't need to work anymore."

Born on February 17, 1902, Marian Anderson grew up in South Philadelphia with her father, John; her mother, Anna; and two sisters, Alyce and Ethel. John Anderson sold ice and coal at the Reading Terminal Market in downtown Philadelphia. Marian was close to her father, whom she later recalled as a tall, dignified man with a lively sense of humor. She was proud of him, especially so on Sundays, when she watched him serve as an usher at the Union Baptist Church.

At the age of six, she found her own place in the church, when she joined the Union Baptist choir. Soon her family and everyone at church recognized her special singing talent. Even as a child Marian loved music. She was eight years old when her father brought home a piano. "When it arrived at our house," she recalled later, "what excitement and joy!" She immediately ran her fingers over the keys, determined that she would learn to play.

When Marian was 10 years old, her father had an accident at work. He was sent home, but instead of regaining his

John Anderson, Marian's father, worked at Philadelphia's Reading Terminal Market (above), but the job he really enjoyed was at the Union Baptist Church, where he served as chief usher.

A black rabbi (the chief religious officer of a Jewish synagogue) prepares to conduct a service in the 1920s. Marian Anderson's grandfather was a devout member of such a congregation.

health, he became increasingly ill. Then the family doctor discovered that John Anderson had developed a brain tumor; he died shortly after Christmas, 1912. "My sisters and I did not put it into so many words," wrote Marian Anderson later, "but we knew that tragedy had moved into our home, and we knew, too, that our lives would change."

After John Anderson's death, his wife and daughters moved in with his parents. Marian's grandfather was a hardworking, deeply religious man. A convert to the Jewish faith, he referred to himself as a Black Jew. His wife was a tall, authoritative woman who, recalled her granddaughter, "liked to remind people that she was part Indian." Grandmother Anderson ruled the household with an iron hand.

Marian continued to sing. Her voice, even when she was very young, was big and free, with a deep, low ring. When she was 13, she was invited to

An early 20th-century women's choir performs in Washington, D.C. Unwelcome in the largely white music schools of the day, many black singers received their musical training in churches.

join the adult choir at her church. She readily accepted but, unwilling to give up any opportunity to sing, she also continued to perform with the junior choir. She remained a member of both groups until she was 20 years old.

Because of the natural depth of her voice, Marian usually sang the alto, or low, parts. If too few men showed up on a Sunday, she could even fill in for them, singing the light tenor, medium baritone, or deep, booming bass parts one octave higher than a male voice. A "range" this wide—the ability to sing many different parts—is unusual, but Marian's was truly exceptional.

As Marian grew up, more and more people acknowledged her extraordinary talent. One of them was Roland Hayes, a famous black tenor who appeared as a guest soloist at the Union Baptist Church. Born in Georgia in

1887, Hayes had studied music at Fisk University in Nashville, Tennessee. In 1911 he had trained with Arthur Hubbard, a renowned voice teacher in Boston, Massachusetts. By 1916 Hayes was recognized as one of the finest singers in America. He was making regular concert appearances around the United States, and he was on the brink of a brilliant international career.

When Hayes came to perform at the Union Baptist Church, the choir director asked Marian to sing on the same program. The invitation was a great honor, but it posed a problem for the needy Anderson family: What could Marian wear?

Understanding Marian's dilemma, church members secretly raised funds to help her meet the great occasion. With the money they gave her—$17.02—Anderson bought a length of white satin, and, with her mother's help, made her first concert gown.

Roland Hayes was amazed by Marian Anderson's voice. After the church concert, he urged her family to send her to Boston to study with his own teacher, Arthur Hubbard. It was an exciting idea, but Marian's grandmother, as the singer later recalled, "was not impressed. So far as she was concerned, I could sing and what was the need of lessons?" The family discussed Hayes's idea for some time, but in the end, the answer was no. "Mother would not oppose Grandmother," noted the singer later, "and Grandmother decided that a young girl should not be sent away from home. To Boston I did not go."

Although Anderson was unable to follow Hayes's advice, he had a strong effect on her career. Many years later, Finnish pianist Kosti Vehanen asked her if she could name any one artist who had particularly inspired her. He recorded her answer in his book, *Marian Anderson: A Portrait*: "I can, definitely," she said. "It was Roland Hayes, whose singing I remember as the most beautiful and inspiring that I had ever heard."

Marian Anderson continued to sing for the sheer joy of it. As the oldest of three girls who had lost their father, however, she felt increasingly responsible for the welfare of her family. She began to accept offers to sing at benefits and church socials.

She was a popular attraction, and her performance fees soon rose from $1.50 to $5. Now she could do what she loved to do and help her family at the same time. Out of each concert fee, she gave $2 to her mother and $1 to each of her sisters, keeping the remaining dollar to cover her own expenses.

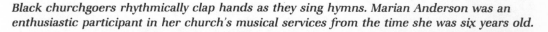

Black churchgoers rhythmically clap hands as they sing hymns. Marian Anderson was an enthusiastic participant in her church's musical services from the time she was six years old.

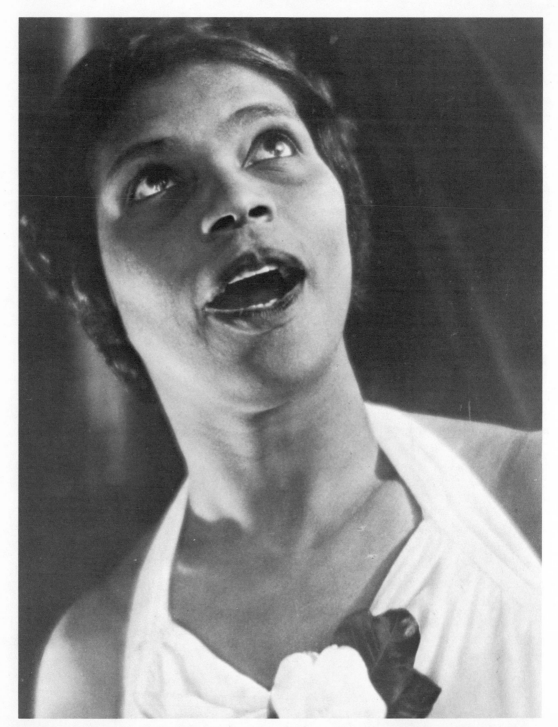

Anderson, who never missed an opportunity to lift her voice in song, did double duty at her church, performing with both the junior and senior choirs.

Thus did Marian Anderson's career begin. Although her dream of going to music school had been thwarted by racism, she was still full of hope about the future. She often thought about what her mother had said after hearing of the school receptionist's crushing words. Her mother had insisted, Anderson wrote in her autobiography, *My Lord, What a Morning*, that "another way would be found to accomplish what might have been accomplished at the conservatory." Her mother had "believed profoundly that somehow someone would be raised up who would be understanding."

Anderson continued to receive strong support from her fellow church members, and Roland Hayes went out of his way to recommend her to concert organizers around Philadelphia. Still, she knew she needed training. Although she loved to sing and had a naturally fine voice, she had not yet developed what performers call *technique*. She had never been taught the mechanics of breath control or how to make her voice move smoothly from low to high notes. She would need these skills to sing the beautiful pieces in French and German that she had heard Roland Hayes perform. While she did not understand the words, she knew these songs were as "soulful" as the hymns and spirituals (traditional songs of American blacks) that she loved so much.

Still the cost of voice lessons remained beyond her means. Then, when Anderson was a junior in high school, she made an important contact. A family friend introduced her to Mary Patterson, a locally famous black soprano who took voice pupils occasionally. Patterson normally charged $1 per lesson, but when she heard Anderson sing, she was so impressed that she offered to teach the young woman without charge.

Hardly able to believe her good fortune, Anderson reported to Patterson's studio. There she listened eagerly as her teacher explained how a singer could project her voice—make it heard to the very back of a theater—without straining it. Patterson also taught her pupil several classical German songs. The two women became good friends; many years later, Anderson was still proudly wearing the dress Patterson had given her from her own wardrobe.

The young singer progressed rapidly, and Patterson soon felt she had taught her all she could. At this point—just before Anderson graduated from high school—another friend was "raised up." This time, it was the school's principal, Dr. Lucy Wilson, who was a great admirer of Anderson and her voice.

Wilson was determined to find the best possible instructor for the young singer. Easily the first choice, she thought, was Giuseppe Boghetti, a

19

Vocal coach Giuseppe Boghetti said he was not interested in new students, but as soon as he heard Anderson sing, he accepted her as a pupil, voluntarily waiving his usual fee.

prominent Italian vocal coach who counted among his former pupils many of the day's finest concert stars. Boghetti was a gruff, unsentimental man, known to be both extremely selective about his students and very difficult to approach. Nevertheless, Wilson managed to get Anderson an appointment to sing for him.

When she arrived for her audition, Anderson was trembling with fright. The great man frowned at her, explained that he was listening to her only as a favor, and told her that he needed no new pupils. He looked at the music she had brought with her— it was the spiritual, "Deep River"—and said he had never heard of it. Closing her eyes, Anderson began to sing, "Deep river, my home is over Jordan. . . ."

She concluded the song and opened her eyes. The room was absolutely silent. Remembering the moment many years afterward, Boghetti said, "When she finished singing 'Deep River,' I just couldn't move." Finally, he turned to Anderson. "I will," he said, "make room for you right away."

Boghetti told Anderson he would need two years to work with her. "After that," he said, "you will be able to go anywhere and sing for anybody." At first, Anderson was overjoyed, but she was soon chilled by the thought of a familiar problem: money.

She earned a small amount from her concerts, but the family needed those funds to supplement her mother's wages as a department-store cleaner. There was certainly no money left over. How could she possibly pay for lessons with Boghetti? It was a fabulous opportunity, but it was, she concluded, beyond her reach. She thanked the famous teacher for his time and prepared to forget the whole idea.

Lucy Wilson, however, had no intention of getting this far and giving up. Thanks to her quiet but persistent efforts, the Union Baptist Church organized a benefit concert at which Roland Hayes himself agreed to perform. The event, which drew a huge crowd, produced more than $600—enough to pay for a whole year of lessons. Anderson began to study with Boghetti at once. (She remained his pupil for the rest of his life, but he never charged for his services after that first year.)

Working with Boghetti meant just that—working, and working hard. Demanding absolute concentration, he put Anderson through a seemingly endless series of vocal and breathing exercises. She began to understand, as she put it in her autobiography, "that the purpose of all the exercises and labors was to give you a thoroughly reliable foundation and to make sure you could do your job under any circumstances. There is no shortcut. You must understand the how and why of what you are doing."

Boghetti taught Anderson a whole new repertoire of songs, many of them operatic arias she had heard Roland Hayes sing. Opera's blend of music and drama enchanted her, and one day she told her teacher she was thinking about concentrating exclusively on it. He made it clear that he disapproved.

At first Anderson was puzzled, but she soon realized why Boghetti discouraged her from considering opera as a career. It was a white world. The Metropolitan Opera Company in New York City, America's foremost stage for the great musical dramas of Verdi, Wagner, Mozart, and Puccini, had never hired a black singer. How could a young woman like Marian Anderson hope to enter a world that barred even such great artists as Roland Hayes?

After she graduated from high school, Anderson had more time to devote to her singing. Now able to accept most of the concert offers she received, she sometimes performed two or three times in the same evening. She had always accompanied herself on the piano, but she knew that if she had an accompanist, she could give her full attention to singing.

One night she met a pianist named Billy King at a concert at the Philadelphia YMCA. King, who was the choirmaster of a Philadelphia Episcopal church, had a solid reputation as one of the area's finest accompanists. Anderson was surprised and pleased when he said he would like to play for her at the concert that night. The two worked well together and soon formed a regular partnership; King would later act as Anderson's manager as well as her accompanist.

Anderson and King soon had all the bookings they could handle. They performed at churches, schools, and private clubs, and they made a series of tours through the South, playing for students at black colleges. As their reputation grew, so did their income. Before long, they were getting $50, then $100 for each performance.

Tenor Roland Hayes was an early admirer and supporter of Marian Anderson. He was among the first black Americans to gain an international reputation as a concert singer.

Anderson's grandparents had always been, as she noted in her autobiography, "kind and loving." Nothing, however, "could take the place of a home of one's own." The family members got along well together, but it had not always been easy to share a house with so many people. Marian Anderson particularly missed having a room where she could sing without bothering anyone. She had often dreamed of having a little house just for her mother, her sisters, and herself.

Thanks to the increased income from her concerts, she was able to make that dream come true. Just before her 20th birthday, she made a down payment on a small house across the street from her grandparents' home. The new place had two bedrooms, one for Marian and Anna Anderson, the other for Alyce and Ethel. It also had an extra bathroom that could be converted into a rehearsal studio.

With a new teacher, a new house, a new accompanist, and a full concert

A 1911 copy of Giacomo Puccini's opera Tosca *shows white performers in the leading roles. The world of opera was tightly closed to black singers until the mid-20th century.*

schedule, Anderson began to stretch out as an artist. "The more I sang," she later wrote about this period, "the more confident I became. . . . My voice was beginning to speak in a new way."

Marian Anderson was a poised and self-confident performer after two years of vocal coaching from Giuseppe Boghetti, but she still felt ill at ease with European classical music.

TWO

The Young Professional

Life on the road was hard for a young black woman in the America of the 1920s, especially in the South. Traveling from town to town on concert trips with Billy King, Anderson repeatedly ran into jim-crow laws—regulations that called for the separation of blacks and whites.

Jim Crow was a character (usually played by a white actor in black makeup) in the popular minstrel shows of the 19th century. His role was to dance to the refrain, "Jump, Jim Crow!" His name, which came to be used as a patronizing term for blacks, was applied to the segregation laws that went into effect after the Civil War.

By 1900 there were jim-crow (for use by blacks only) cars on trains, jim-crow entrances and seats in theaters, jim-crow drinking fountains in city parks. Blacks were barred from white-owned restaurants and hotels, and schools and residential areas were strictly segregated by race.

Jim-crow laws had been declared legal by the United States Supreme Court in its 1896 "separate but equal" decision. This ruling permitted segregation if the facilities used by each race were of equal quality. In fact, however, the facilities available to blacks were almost always inferior to those used by whites—and sometimes, blacks had none at all.

On railroads, for example, the dining cars were reserved for whites. Blacks making long trips by rail were obliged to bring their food with them or to eat the stale, overpriced sandwiches sold in the aisles of the train. One day Anderson and King were on their way to an evening engagement in the South. Knowing there would be no time to eat after they left the train, King introduced himself and Anderson to the

Under the South's so-called Jim Crow laws, blacks were restricted to "separate but equal" facilities everywhere — even in parking lots — during much of the 20th century.

Wearing "blackface" makeup, white entertainers take part in a minstrel show. The source of "Jim Crow," a derogatory term for blacks, these shows were hugely popular in 19th-century America.

porter, who was black, and asked if it would be possible to get a hot dinner.

The pair had become famous in the black community, and the porter recognized them at once. He was eager to do what he could to make such important artists comfortable. Leading them into the dining car before the regular mealtime, he seated them at the curtained-off table normally used by the waiters. There he served them a delicious, hot meal.

"There were extra things at our table, and even extra-large portions," Anderson recalled later. "This was their way of saying that they were glad we had had the courage to come back and be served." She gave the porter her most dazzling smile. Even though she and King were not seated as "equals," she knew the porter had risked his job to accommodate them.

Sometimes racial discrimination was open—"Whites Only" signs were all too common. Sometimes it was subtle—a black might wait to be served by a storekeeper until long after all the whites had been waited on. Anderson once said, "Sometimes it's like having a hair across your cheek. You can't find it with your hand, but you keep brushing at it because the feel of it is irritating."

Anderson found racial prejudice puzzling as well as "irritating." In her autobiography she wrote, "If one only searched one's heart one would know that none of us is responsible for the complexion of his skin, and that we could not change it if we wished to, and many of us don't wish to, and that this fact of nature offers no clue to the character or quality of the person underneath."

Anderson and King continued to travel though the South, making many concert appearances at such black colleges as Hampton Institute in Virginia and Howard University in Washington, D.C. Acting as Anderson's manager as well as her accompanist, King arranged most of the bookings through people he had met when he had accompanied Roland Hayes on tour.

Hayes himself continued to boost Anderson's career. The celebrated tenor, who had made his first European tour in 1921, and who would, in 1923, become the first black singer to appear at prestigious Carnegie Hall in New York City, recommended Anderson and King to the many concert organizers he knew.

When Anderson was 20, she met a tall young art student named Orpheus Fisher at a postconcert reception in Wilmington, Delaware. A few weeks later, Fisher—known to his friends as "King"—showed up at Anderson's house in Philadelphia. He had clearly been impressed with the Philadelphia singer, and she found him interesting, as well.

Fisher became a frequent caller at Anderson's home and often wrote to her when she was on the road. After he moved to New York to continue his studies, one of his letters posed a novel question: Why shouldn't the two of them send their clothes to the laundry in the same bundle?

He was, of course, proposing mar-

An irate train conductor orders a black passenger to leave a "white only" car in 1856. Conditions had changed little by the 1920s, when Marian Anderson began to tour the South.

riage, but Anderson gently turned him down. It would not be fair, she said, for her to become his wife at a time when her career was her chief passion. The young man gave in, but he did not give up. Marian Anderson had not seen the last of Orpheus Fisher.

After two years of study with Giuseppe Boghetti, Anderson's self-confidence had increased dramatically. She and King began to make appearances in theaters and small concert halls as well as in churches and schools. Their audiences included music lovers of all races, and critics started to review their performances in some national publications.

Anderson's repertoire was also increasing in scope. She still sang the hymns and spirituals on which she was beginning to build her reputation, but now her programs included some of the beautiful classical pieces she had first heard sung by Roland Hayes. She sang works by Franz Schubert and Johannes Brahms, as well as pieces written by Russian, French, and Italian composers. Although she could interpret the music of these songs flawlessly, she had to learn the lyrics syllable by syllable, because she understood no French, German, or Italian.

In 1923 Anderson competed in a vocal contest sponsored by the Philharmonic Society of Philadelphia. The judges, deeply impressed by her extraordinary voice, broke with tradition and awarded her first prize; it was the first time a black singer had won the contest. Anderson followed up this triumph by performing with the Philadelphia Orchestra in a concert that was heard by thousands of people over a new entertainment medium: radio.

The singer's next important appearance was in New York City's Harlem, where she performed before a standing-room-only audience in late 1923. Convinced by Anderson's Harlem success that she could draw an equally enthusiastic crowd of white New Yorkers, the impresario (organizer) who had arranged the Harlem recital proposed a recital at Manhattan's famous Town Hall.

Such a concert would be a major step in Anderson's career. At the age of 22, she would be one of the youngest soloists to perform in the celebrated concert space as well as one of the few

White patrons enjoy a floor show at Harlem's popular Cotton Club in the 1920s. It was this form of entertainment — not classical music — that the era's whites expected from black performers.

blacks to have performed there. It would, however, be a gamble: Anderson would have to finance the recital herself, hoping, of course, that her investment would be repaid by the sale of tickets. On the other hand, if New York's music critics liked her performance, her prestige—and her future concert fees—would be substantially increased.

After weighing the pros and cons of this important decision with her mother, her accompanist, and her teacher, Anderson decided to take the risk. The concert was booked into Town Hall for April 25, 1924.

She rehearsed for the event for months, planning a long and demanding program. Along with a scattering of spirituals, it would include works by English, Russian, Italian, German, and Bohemian composers. Among them were Schubert, Brahms, George Frederick Handel, Nikolay Rimsky-Korsakov, Sergey Rachmaninoff, Gaetano Donizetti, Giovanni Pergolesi, Richard Strauss, and Antonín Dvořák.

Traditional Town Hall audiences were largely white. Anderson was not unknown in New York—she had appeared not only at the recent Harlem recital but at a Baptist church convention and at a big meeting of the National Association for the Advancement of Colored People (NAACP)—but the bulk of her listeners had been black. Still, she and King felt that they had made enough impression on the white

New York City's Town Hall is pictured on the program for Marian Anderson's disastrous 1924 concert. The young singer was deeply depressed by the recital's critical and financial failure.

community to attract at least a respectable crowd to Town Hall. They were wrong.

So few people had showed up by curtain time that the impresario delayed the concert's opening for half an hour, hoping for late arrivals. None came. Anderson and King walked onto the stage and faced an auditorium peopled only by a handful of listeners in the front and back rows.

King seated himself at the keyboard and began to play. Anderson closed her eyes and sang. The tiny audience applauded after each song, but Anderson knew she was not doing her best work. She was especially displeased with her rendition of the Brahms *lied* (poem set to music); German had always been the language in which she was least comfortable. A short review in the next day's newspaper confirmed her self-criticism. "Marian Anderson," said the article, "sang her Brahms as if by rote [mechanically]." From start to finish then, the concert had been a disaster.

Anderson was not a woman easily discouraged, but the Town Hall experience was a heavy blow. She felt she had failed all the people who believed in her—her family, Boghetti, King, her fellow church members. She returned to Philadelphia dejected and doubtful that she should continue to pursue a singing career. For several months, she neither sang nor played; she spent most of her time alone, barely speaking even to her patient mother.

"Whatever you do in this world, no matter how good it is, you will never be able to please everybody," her mother told her. "All you can strive for is to do the best it is humanly possible for you to do."

As it turned out, it was her mother who pulled her out of her depression—but not through her words of wisdom and consolation. Anna Anderson, still working long, exhausting hours at the Philadelphia department store, had come home one evening ill and feverish. Her daughters called the family doctor, who ordered her to stay in bed for several days. Nevertheless, she was up and dressed for work the following morning.

Marian Anderson respected her mother's independence, and she knew the family still depended on her wages, but this was too much. She called her mother's boss, identified herself, and said, "I just wanted to tell you that Mother will not be coming back to work."

Anna Anderson protested, but her daughter was firm. She was, she said, going back to her singing immediately, and she was going to make enough money so that her mother would never have to work again. Marian Anderson then called Billy King and said she was ready to pick up her career where she had left it before the calamitous Town Hall concert.

King began to organize a performance schedule and Anderson went back to Boghetti's studio. Town Hall had shown her that she still had much to learn—for one thing, foreign languages. She would have to become fluent in German, French, and Italian, the languages necessary to every classical vocalist.

Anderson knew that song is poetry, and that poetry is language. It was not enough to look up foreign words in a dictionary and to approximate the sounds. Until she understood the subtle meanings and exact pronunciation of the words, she could not properly deliver a song to her audience. So, while Boghetti worked with her on Italian, she studied French with a local high school teacher. She started looking for a German instructor—and she entered another singing contest.

Vocal coach Frank La Forge was "a charming man" and "a good musician," noted Anderson. Her decision to study with him, however, infuriated her longtime teacher, Giuseppe Boghetti.

This competition, sponsored by the National Music League, was held in New York City. It offered a tempting first prize: the chance to perform as soloist with the New York Philharmonic Orchestra, conducted by Willem van Hoogstraten. The winner's performance would be given at a concert in Lewisohn Stadium, an immense, open-air Manhattan theater.

Anderson went to New York with Boghetti to try out for the contest. She was one of 300 hopeful singers from all over the United States. Each was given a number; when that number was called over the loudspeaker, the contestant would come to the stage and sing until the judges rang a bell. There was, cautioned the judges, to be absolutely no applause.

Anderson was nervous; her self-con-fidence had been severely shaken by the Town Hall fiasco. She became even more tense when she heard six contestants sing "O Mio Fernando," an aria from the Donizetti opera, *La Favorita*. It was the song she had picked for her own demonstration. As she waited her turn to sing, she saw one contestant after another walk dejectedly from the stage after the heartbreaking sound of the judges' bell.

Finally, her number was called. Boghetti wished her luck, and she walked slowly to the stage. She began to sing, one part of her mind "waiting apprehensively," as she later recalled, "for the voice of doom." Hearing no such voice—or bell—Anderson finished the aria, her pronunciation of its Italian words much improved after Boghetti's language lessons. She was the first contestant who had been allowed to complete a song, and the auditorium, filled with contenders, teachers, and accompanists, erupted in a storm of applause.

The voice of one of the judges boomed through the hall. "*Quiet!* No applause!" Hands continued to clap as Anderson bowed and walked away from center stage. She was stopped by the voice on the loudspeaker: "Does the contestant have another song?" Anderson gave the pianist a sheet of music and sang an encore.

A few days later, Boghetti got a phone call: Anderson had been named as one of the 16 semifinalists in the contest. This group would sing, then be narrowed down to four finalists, one of whom would wind up as the winner.

Anderson sang three selections in the semifinal round, then returned with Boghetti to his New York studio. This time, the telephone was ringing when they got there. Anderson described the moment in her autobiography: "When Mr. Boghetti hung up he rushed to me in excitement. 'We have won,' he shouted. 'There will be no finals!'"

The evening of the Lewisohn Stadium concert—August 26, 1925—was balmy and clear. The sky was beginning to fill with stars as Anderson walked onstage to join the conductor. Every seat in the huge amphitheater was filled. There were many blacks in the crowd—among them, Anderson's family and friends from Philadelphia— and many whites, too. Anderson had never before sung with a full symphony orchestra, but she sensed waves of good will emanating from the crowd, and she was calm.

Conductor van Hoogstraten tapped his baton, and the audience settled back in silent expectation. Pure and rich, Anderson's strong contralto poured into the night sky. The last notes of "O Mio Fernando" gave way to a thunderous roar of approval from almost 8,000 throats. From the stage came a special tribute: the staccato tapping of musicians' bows on their music stands.

For her encore, Anderson was accompanied by Billy King as she sang a group of spirituals: "Deep River," "Heav'n, Heav'n" and "Song of the Heart." She sang far past the concert's scheduled closing time, as the audience demanded one encore after another. "As I sang I felt at ease," she later reported. "I like to believe," she added with characteristic modesty, "that the performance was not too bad."

This time, the newspaper reviews were different. "Miss Anderson made an excellent impression," said the *New York Times*. "She is endowed by nature with a voice of unusual compass, color, and dramatic capability."

Said the New York *Herald Tribune*: "A remarkable voice was heard last night at Lewisohn Stadium. Its possessor was Marian Anderson...." Although this review contained high praise for the richness and power of Anderson's voice, it struck an all too familar note: She was good, it implied, *in spite of* being "a young Negro."

The success of the stadium concert had a marked effect on Anderson and King's concert tours. The following fall, they were invited to perform in California and Canada, and they began to see more and more white faces at their concerts. Even in the usually segregated South, noted the singer in her autobiography, "When there was a concert in a Negro school auditorium, there would be white people in the audience." The pair's fees also improved:

Born to a former slave in 1888, choir leader Hall Johnson (center) was an authority on Negro spirituals. Anderson sang with his highly respected group at Manhattan's Carnegie Hall in 1925.

Now they were receiving from $350 to $500 for each appearance.

Not long after the stadium concert, Anderson was invited to appear as a soloist with the Hall Johnson Choir, a well-known group of black singers, at New York's Carnegie Hall. They performed to a large, enthusiastic audience, and afterward, one listener came backstage. He introduced himself to Anderson as Arthur Judson, president of one of the country's most prominent concert-management bureaus.

When Judson told Anderson he would like her to join the group of distinguished musicians he represented, she was both flattered and excited. Association with an agency like Judson's

might give her career a major boost, and the concert fees he could obtain were bound to be higher than those she had been receiving. She agreed to meet him at his Philadelphia office a few days later.

With Boghetti at her side, Anderson entered Judson's office, where impressive, autographed photographs of some of the country's leading singers covered the walls. Boghetti was slightly uncomfortable with the smooth-talking manager, but the contract Judson offered seemed like a good one, and Anderson ended the meeting by becoming a "Judson artist."

Anderson's new association did not provide a fast route to success. The agency did obtain higher fees for her, but because fewer institutions were able to afford them, that meant fewer bookings. Furthermore, there were new expenses: Anderson had to pay for the costly programs and brochures issued by the Judson office, and, she noted, "I had to have more than one evening dress."

Although she was cautious about spending large sums on her wardrobe, Anderson began, she wrote, "to realize how important one's appearance was. I think that my people felt a sense of pride in seeing me dressed well.... It made them feel good, I found out, to see one of their own pleasantly got up."

Arthur Judson was the head of a prestigious concert-management bureau. He offered Marian Anderson a contract after hearing her sing with the Hall Johnson Choir.

About a year after she signed with concert manager Judson, he made a suggestion that justified Boghetti's suspicions about him. Judson advised Anderson to start studying with a different vocal coach, Frank La Forge of New York City. La Forge had an excellent reputation for his work with young singers, and he had connections in the music world that would undoubtedly prove helpful.

Anderson decided to follow Judson's recommendation and work with La Forge for a year. When Boghetti was told about the plan, he was furious. He insisted, she recalled later, that "there was nothing that I could get in any other studio that I could not get from him." She explained that she planned to continue studying with him as well, but Boghetti indignantly rejected the idea. "He would not have me," she noted sadly. "It was only later, when the lessons with Mr. La Forge had stopped, that Mr. Boghetti relented and let me return to his studio."

La Forge, who was a noted pianist and composer as well as a teacher, found Anderson an eager and pliable student. The two got along well, but after a year, Anderson was still unable to master the German *lieder* (the plural of lied) she wanted so badly to sing.

At one small recital in La Forge's studio, she sang a German song and mixed up the words. The people in the audience, she noted, "were gracious, but the incident disturbed me. It kept

Anderson models one of the gowns she bought for her Judson-agency concert tours. She said her favorite dresses were "simple in design but made of good material and effective in appearance."

haunting me and making me feel that I must find some way to become absolutely sure of my German." She decided to go to Europe.

Arthur Judson wanted Anderson to continue to build her reputation at home, and he was dismayed by her proposed trip. "If you go to Europe," he told her, "it will only be to satisfy your vanity." Her mind was made up. "I will go, then, for that purpose," she replied.

Anderson's other colleagues were more encouraging. Her mother applauded her plan, as did Boghetti, La Forge, and Billy King. Her friend Lawrence Brown, a fine pianist who had traveled abroad with Roland Hayes, advised her to go to England. There, he said, she could meet Raimund von Zur Mühlen, one of the world's foremost teachers of lieder. Brown wrote Anderson a letter of introduction to von Zur Mühlen, and Billy King wrote to Roger Quilter, a wealthy British composer known for his willingness to help young musicians.

Anderson wanted to go abroad for several reasons. One, of course, was to learn German and improve her French and Italian. She also felt the need for change. "I was going stale," she wrote later. "I had to get away from my old haunts for a while; progress was at a standstill; repeating the same engagements each year, even if programs varied a little, was becoming routine; my career needed a fresh impetus [boost], and perhaps a European stamp would help."

Anderson, now 27 years old, sailed for England aboard the ocean liner *Ile de France* in the summer of 1929. The journey would be interesting, but not, unfortunately, as productive as she expected it to be.

Traveling on the French ship gave Anderson her first taste of a foreign culture, which both excited and intimidated her. In her autobiography, she recalled an exchange with a dining room waiter early in the voyage. She had requested that her steak be well done, then had smilingly declined a glass of wine. Overcooked beef was bad enough, but refusing wine? The waiter was clearly horrified. "You could never be the wife of a Frenchman!" he said. Anderson was amused. "I suppose," she observed, "that to him this was the worst that could happen to anyone."

Things started going awry almost as soon as she landed in England. First she learned that composer Roger Quilter, who had offered her a room in his home, had suddenly gone into the hospital. Instead she went to stay with an American friend's family, but when she got there, she realized she had lost her music case, which contained not only music but all her money. The case was finally recovered, and she set out by train for Sussex, the home of Raimund von Zur Mühlen. The master of the lied

Composer Roger Quilter, whom Anderson described as "an English-looking Englishman," arranged a recital for her in 1930. It was politely received, but failed to advance her career.

American pianist Lawrence Brown joins German voice teacher Raimund von Zur Mühlen (left) in an English garden. Following Brown's advice, Anderson visited von Zur Mühlen in 1929.

Impresario Sol Hurok (right) greets one of his famous clients, opera star Fyodor Chaliapin. Hoping Hurok would agree to manage her, Anderson tried to contact him in 1930, but he never called back.

was by then old and feeble; after only two brief sessions with Anderson, he became too ill to teach anyone.

Anderson spent the rest of her time in England working with two competent but uninspired voice teachers and attending concerts and social gatherings. When Roger Quilter recovered, he introduced her to his musical friends and arranged a recital for her at a London theater, Wigmore Hall. Her appearance was greeted with warm applause and friendly press reviews, but it led to nothing further. At last, after a year abroad, Anderson sailed for home.

"When I returned to the United States I had no big achievements to show for my absence," she wrote later. "If I had done something noteworthy, such as singing for the king and queen, that might have made a difference. But Wigmore Hall? That was just another appearance by an American aspirant. To people who wanted to know what had been accomplished abroad, there was not a great deal to tell."

Soon after her return to Philadelphia, Anderson had a caller; it was "King" Fisher, obviously still interested in joint bundles of laundry. Anderson was delighted to see her tall, handsome admirer, but she was still not ready to consider marriage. She avoided the subject, talking animatedly about her year abroad instead. Once again, Fisher walked away. "I could not tell," wrote Anderson, "whether I would ever see him again." She was a determined woman. Perhaps she had not yet noticed that King Fisher had the same quality.

The trip to Europe had little impact on Anderson's career. The bookings lined up by the Judson agency were disappointingly familiar: concerts in small recital halls, churches, and schools. "The sensation that I was standing still, which had led to my going to England, returned," she wrote.

Perhaps, she thought, she should try a change in management.

Anderson knew that a Russian-born concert manager named Sol Hurok had become one of America's foremost impresarios. Hurok had introduced such legendary performers as ballerina Anna Pavlova, opera singer Fyodor Chaliapin, and violinist Efrem Zimbalist. He was also known to be receptive to "undiscovered" talent. Anderson placed several calls to his office, but they were not returned; apparently, he was not interested in managing her.

She knew she had to do something to move her career off the plateau where it seemed to have settled. She decided to return to Europe, this time to Germany, where she could learn the language and the lieder. How she would finance the trip, she did not know, but, as she wrote later, "I knew I must go, and I believed that a way would be found."

After giving a concert in Chicago in 1931, Anderson was approached by a representative from the Julius Rosenwald Fund, a foundation set up by a wealthy Chicago businessman to advance higher education for blacks. The fund representative complimented her on her performance and then asked her about her plans for the future. She told him she "wanted and needed" to study in Germany.

Anderson was exactly the kind of person the foundation aimed at assisting, and she was quickly awarded

Crossing the Atlantic for the second time, Anderson heads for Germany in 1931. On this visit, she was determined to master the German lieder (art songs) she had loved since childhood.

a fellowship. "This was heartening," remembered the singer. "As Mother would say, a way had been found." She was soon aboard a German steamship, her destination, Berlin.

Anderson rehearses with vocal coach Michael Raucheisen during her 1931 visit to Germany. A specialist in lieder, Raucheisen helped Anderson polish her German diction.

THREE

Europe: A Warm Reception

By the time Marian Anderson sailed for Europe in 1931, almost six years had passed since her appearance with the New York Philharmonic at Lewisohn Stadium. Her career had advanced very little in that period, but now things would begin to change—rapidly.

In Berlin she took a room with a family that spoke only German. This arrangement was just what she needed to learn the language of lieder, but there were some confusing moments at the beginning. At one point, she recalled, she thought she was being asked if she would like some "chicken in a glass"—a dish that turned out to be eggs sunny-side up. "I quickly acquired a pocket dictionary," she wrote, "and resorted to it at every impasse. We all used grunts and groans and gestures, and somehow we understood each other."

Once established in her new residence, Anderson began to take German lessons and to study lieder with Michael Raucheisen, a German vocal coach who had been recommended to her. Slowly her confidence grew. Finally she felt ready to sing before a German audience, so she asked a local concert manager about arranging a recital.

The manager, recalled Anderson in her autobiography, "told me that I must be presented properly, adding significantly that he understood that I had a lot of money behind me. I assured him that he was perfectly right: there was a lot of money behind me, so far behind that it would never catch up with me!"

Despite the humorous reference to her tight budget, Anderson decided to pay for a recital at Berlin's celebrated concert hall, the Bachsaal. Accompanied by Raucheisen, her teacher, she

Horse-drawn wagons and motorcars share a Berlin thoroughfare in the early 1930s. Unable to speak German when she arrived in 1931, Anderson said she communicated with "grunts and groans and gestures."

sang a group of songs by Beethoven and Schubert, followed by a selection of spirituals. The audience, she noted, reacted "kindly" to the American songs.

The newspaper reviews were complimentary, but not wildly enthusiastic. Still, she was pleased and relieved that a German audience, "a group that [was] alert to every subtlety of its own language and [that knew] most of the lieder by heart," had received her with obvious respect.

One day she was working on a new song with Raucheisen when two strangers appeared at the studio. They identified themselves as Rulle Rasmussen, a Norwegian concert manager, and Kosti Vehanen, a Finnish pianist. They explained that they were touring Europe, looking for new talent. Anderson invited them to her next concert, where Vehanen was stunned by her singing. He later recalled telling Rasmussen, "I can't forget the colors in her voice—not only one color, but hundreds. If she succeeds in using all those colors to deepen the meaning of each word, she will be marvelous."

Soon after the Scandinavians had left Berlin, they sent Anderson an official invitation to perform in Oslo, Norway; Stockholm, Sweden; and Helsinki, Finland. She accepted at once. Her first major concert of the tour was in Oslo, where Anderson so dazzled the audience that a second concert was immediately scheduled.

Norwegians, noted Anderson with amusement, "were not accustomed to Negroes." One reviewer described her as being "dressed in electric-blue satin and looking very much like a chocolate bar." Another said she was "like *café au lait* [coffee with milk]." These comments, said the singer, "had nothing to do with any prejudice; they expressed a kind of wonder."

After Norway Anderson headed for Sweden, where she met Helmer Enwall, a Swedish concert manager who would prove to be very important to her career. Audience reaction at the two concerts Enwall arranged in Stockholm was, as the singer put it, "reserved," especially when compared with the approval displayed by the Norwegians.

Enwall assured Anderson that she had been successful, that the Swedes "were slow to manifest their warmth," and that they would eventually acclaim her. She had her doubts, but she proceeded with the tour, going on to Helsinki, Finland. Here she would be accompanied by Kosti Vehanen, the Finnish pianist she had met in Berlin.

In his book, *Marian Anderson: A Portrait*, Vehanen wrote about his first rehearsal with the singer. Her voice, he said, made him think "of an exquisite flower that stands alone in a deep forest.... The sound I heard swelled to majestic power, the flower opened its petals to full brilliance, and I was enthralled by one of nature's rare wonders."

Anderson admired Vehanen in return. He was, she noted in her autobiography, "a man of culture and a gentleman." He was also a first-class musician, and he was familiar with the lieder that Anderson so much wanted to master. Vehanen played for her for the rest of her tour and eventually became her regular accompanist. "He helped me a great deal," she said, "in guiding me onto the path that led to my becoming an accepted international singer."

Anderson's scheduled six months in Europe were drawing to a close, and she prepared to go home. She had spent only a few weeks in Scandinavia, but the visit had made a tremendous difference in her life. Being accepted by the audiences in these countries made her realize, she wrote later, "that the time and energy invested in seeking to become an artist were worthwhile, and that what I had dared to aspire to was not impossible."

Anderson inspects a snowman during her first trip to Sweden in 1931. Initially cool to the American singer, Swedes later came to idolize her, reporting an epidemic of "Marian fever."

Anderson hoped that her success in Scandinavia would make a difference in the attitude of managers and audiences at home, but once again, she was disappointed. If she had been well received in Paris or London, she was told, Americans would be impressed, but success in Scandinavia meant little. Her bookings continued to be in modest recital halls and schools.

One day, soon after her return to the United States, she received a cablegram from Swedish concert manager Helmer Enwall. It said, *Can offer you 20 concerts. When can you come?* While she was deciding what to do, another cable arrived: *Can offer 40 concerts.* Then came a third: *Can offer you 60.* Anderson was both pleased and amused by Enwall's urgent tone. "If I had not known him to be so utterly reliable," she wrote later, "I might have thought that he was going wild with a kind of personal numbers game."

She sent a reply explaining that she was committed to a number of American appearances. When they were over, she would be happy to accept Enwall's first offer of 20 concerts. He quickly agreed. Anderson then asked for and got another Rosenwald scholarship. In 1933 she was on her way to Europe for the third time.

Enwall was as good as his word. He had booked even more dates for Anderson than he promised; within the next 12 months, she would give 108 concerts throughout Norway, Sweden,

Finland, and Denmark. Accompanied by Vehanen, she played to packed houses everywhere, generating the same enthusiasm as she had earlier—with one exception. Things were different in Sweden.

In that chilly country, Anderson noted, "The reserve seemed to have melted." She got letters containing such messages as, "We wanted to be sure, and now we are sure," or "Pardon us for being slow to recognize." The delighted singer said that once the Swedes opened themselves to her, "they embraced me wholeheartedly. The newspapers ran caricatures, photographs, all sorts of articles about me. One piece went so far as to term the whole thing 'Marian fever.'"

Among Anderson's newer selections were several songs by Jean Sibelius, the Finnish composer who was so popular with his compatriots that his birthday was celebrated as a national holiday. The Finns applauded Anderson's renditions of Sibelius's works, but the songs were extremely difficult to sing, and she was not convinced she was doing them justice.

One day, to Anderson's amazement, Vehanen told her he had arranged a meeting with the great Sibelius himself. She could sing for him, and then she would learn whether or not she had the right approach to his music. When she arrived for the appointment, Anderson's nervousness about meeting the celebrated composer intensified.

Pianist Kosti Vehanen (left) visits Finnish composer Jean Sibelius and his wife in the 1930s. Awed by Anderson's voice, Sibelius dedicated one of his songs, "Solitude," to her.

"With his strong head and broad shoulders," she recalled later, "he looked like a figure carved out of granite."

Sibelius suggested that Anderson sing a few songs. Then, he said, they would have coffee. Vehanen began to play, Anderson sang, and Sibelius listened. One of her pieces was "Norden," the Sibelius song she loved best. But what, she kept wondering, would he think of her interpretation of his music? In her autobiography, Anderson described what happened next.

"When I was finished [Sibelius] arose, strode to my side, and threw his arms around me in a hearty embrace. 'My roof is too low for you,' he said, and then he called out in a loud voice

It was in Paris that Anderson finally met impresario Sol Hurok. Both excited and terrified by the encounter, she said it made her feel "like a marathon runner at the end of his race."

people who did come cheered loudly. The second concert was sold out; apparently the patrons of the first had spread the word.

By the time of her third concert, crowds of would-be attendees were being turned away from the box office. During the intermission at this performance, the local concert manager appeared at the door of Anderson's dressing room with a visitor: Sol Hurok.

Hurok was the powerful impresario Anderson had tried—and failed—to meet in the United States. Regarded by many as a genius, he was among the most influential theatrical producers and managers in the world. Now he was here, here in Marian Anderson's Paris dressing room—here to meet *her*!

He had, he said, been passing the theater earlier in the day and had seen that an American singer—unknown to him—was performing there. His curiosity piqued, he had arranged to get a ticket. Although he made no comment on Anderson's singing, he asked if she could meet with him the next day. "Could I!" wrote Anderson in her autobiography. "I don't know how I got through the rest of the program!"

When she went to Hurok's office with Vehanen, she was terrified. "I cannot tell you how big and important he seemed to me; Kosti and I felt inadequate in his presence," she wrote. "I think I would have run away if I had dared."

Hurok still said nothing about An-

to his wife, 'Not coffee, but champagne!' " It was a moment neither Anderson nor Vehanen would ever forget.

Sibelius kept the singer and her accompanist for much longer than the half hour he had promised. He talked, explained, played, listened, advised. "I left feeling a glow from the meeting with so great a man," said Anderson later. "It was as if a veil had been lifted."

Not long after Anderson met Sibelius, Enwall booked three concert appearances for her in Paris. The first was rather sparsely attended, although the derson's singing, but in his memoir, *Impresario*, he described his first reaction to her voice: "Chills danced up my spine and my palms were wet." At the meeting, he asked a few questions about her concert experience, and then he said exactly what she had been hoping he would: "I might be able to do something for you."

Hurok offered Anderson a contract for 15 concerts, which she signed as soon she could arrange a release from the Judson agency. Before she returned to the United States as a Hurok artist, however, she had to fulfill the commitments she had made to sing in several European cities, including Geneva, Switzerland; Brussels, Belgium; and Vienna and Salzburg in Austria.

The concert in Vienna held special meaning for Anderson, because the Austrian capital had been the home of Franz Schubert, one of the composers she loved best. Although Schubert had lived for only 31 years (from 1797 until 1828), he had composed more than 600 lieder, as well as 8 symphonies and many other works. His musical setting for "Ave Maria," which Anderson always treasured, eventually became one of her "trademarks."

From there, it was on to Salzburg, where Anderson was scheduled to sing in the Grand Ballroom of the Hôtel de l'Europe on August 28, 1935. Just before the concert, she was told that Arturo Toscanini, one of the world's most celebrated conductors, might attend. "I

Austrian composer Franz Schubert wrote hundreds of songs, each, said Anderson, "more beautiful than the last." Her only problem, she added, was deciding which ones to sing.

was hoping he would not," she wrote later. "I held him in such high esteem that I felt I could not do anything of interest to him."

But Toscanini did come to the concert, making Anderson, she recalled afterward, "nervous as a beginner." Swallowing her fear, she began her program, which was largely composed of spirituals. Few members of the audience understood the words of the songs, but they were transfixed by her performance.

Vincent Sheean, an American journalist who was at the concert, later wrote that when she finished "The Crucifixion," there was "no applause at all—a silence instinctive, natural,

47

Anderson was critically applauded for her delivery of German lieder, but her admirers were usually more moved by her emotional renditions of spirituals such as "The Crucifixion."

Conductor Arturo Toscanini displays his legendary skill with a baton. Anderson was stunned by his comment about her. "Yours is a voice," he said, "one hears once in a hundred years."

and intense, so that you were afraid to breathe. What Anderson had done was something outside the limits of classical or romantic music: She frightened us with the conception . . . of a mighty suffering."

Then, at the end of the concert, Arturo Toscanini came backstage. The conductor took Anderson's hand and spoke in a low voice. "The sight of him," wrote Anderson, "caused my heart to leap and throb so violently I did not hear a word he said. All I could do was mumble a thank you, sir, thank you very much, and then he left."

The other people present later told Anderson what Toscanini had said to her: "Yours is a voice one hears once in a hundred years." She was overcome. One of the greatest conductors of all time had told her she possessed the voice of the century!

After she had made several more European appearances, Anderson knew it was time to return to the United States. Hurok had arranged a recital in New York City's Town Hall for December 30, and besides, she had been away from home for two years.

A number of people asked her, then and later, why she did not remain in Europe. She had not only earned a solid reputation there, she had been accepted as a human being; there was little trace in Europe of the racial prejudice so prevalent in America. About settling in Europe, she later said, "No such thought ever entered my mind."

She had, she said, "gone to Europe to achieve something, to reach for a place as a serious artist." But ultimately, she declared, "I was—and am—an American. I wanted to come home, and I knew that I had to test myself as a serious artist in my own country."

Before she came home from Europe in 1935, Anderson struggled with a difficult question: Would her appearance with a white accompanist be seen as disloyalty to her race?

FOUR

Home

Eleven years after her disastrous 1924 concert, Marian Anderson returned to Manhattan's Town Hall in triumph. Reviewing her December 30, 1935, performance in the *New York Times*, critic Howard Taubman called her "one of the great singers of our time," and "the possessor of an excelling voice and art." He compared her with Joe Louis, the black boxer who would soon become heavyweight champion of the world. Both, he noted, had grown up poor; both had become successful by developing their "natural endowments."

"If Joe Louis," said Taubman, "deserves to be an American hero for bowling over a lot of pushovers, then Marian Anderson has the right to at least a comparable standing. Handel, Schubert, and Sibelius are not pushovers."

Anderson had faced a number of problems on her way to Town Hall.

First had been the question of her accompanist—Kosti Vehanen was white. Many people, including Anderson's mother, felt that she owed it to her race to appear with a black accompanist, either Billy King or another American pianist. Writing to her daughter during the summer before the concert, Anna Anderson had made her position clear.

"There has never been one of our race to attain such heights, to be so highly acclaimed and so universally beloved as yourself," she wrote, "so I pray that you may not throw a blanket over all you have done by bringing one of another race to work with you."

Anderson realized that no matter what decision she made, she would displease someone. "If I did not use Billy King," she wrote in her autobiography, "some of my own people might be offended. And particularly in the South, where I knew I would be sing-

Anna Anderson, a thoughtful woman with a deep sense of pride in her people, believed that her daughter should select a black pianist for her American concert appearances.

ing, people might take offense that a white man was serving as my accompanist."

On the other hand, she reasoned, "Because I had been working most recently with Kosti, I felt more at home with him in the new programs. With his help I had made considerable progress in the weaker phases of my repertory."

Vehanen himself was eager to accompany his friend to her homeland, even after she warned him that his presence might cause resentment.

"Marian," she quoted him as saying humorously, "if I can come and play only the first pieces on the program, I will charm them so that they will want me to stay."

Anderson finally made the hard choice. She had always believed that her musical abilities were gifts from God, and that it was her job to see that they were used effectively. "I knew in my heart," she wrote, "that the right decision would be the one taken on musical grounds." She also knew that Billy King would understand and respect whatever decision she made. When she left Europe for the United States in mid-December, Kosti Vehanen sailed with her.

Aboard the *Ile de France*, Anderson ran into a familiar irritation. The first day out, reported Vehanen in his memoirs, an elegantly dressed white woman stared at the singer and then wondered—loudly—where "that poor girl" would be seated for her meals.

A nearby ship's officer made it clear that Anderson had been assigned to a prominent table in the ship's main dining room. The inquiring lady, he said, was free to request a table in one of the smaller rooms. After she had stalked off, the officer apologized to Anderson for the breach of etiquette. Anderson smiled and gave him her customary response to such situations: "That's all right. She didn't know any better."

Anderson's second major problem

had nothing to do with prejudice. Making her way down a stairway one day when the sea was rough, she lost her balance and fell, hurting her ankle. Without x-ray equipment, the ship's doctor could do little more than bandage the ankle and advise the patient to keep off her feet.

When she reached Philadelphia, Anderson's family and friends greeted her with a welcome-home party so exciting that she almost forgot about the pain. The next day, however, her ankle was worse; x-rays revealed it was broken. Her doctor fitted her with a heavy plaster cast from foot to knee; she would, he said, have to wear it for six weeks. But the Town Hall concert was only six days away!

Some advisers suggested that Anderson postpone the concert, but she knew Sol Hurok had invited all the top music critics, distributed posters, paid for advertisements, and printed programs. Putting her crutches and wheelchair in a car, she went to New York City. Hurok tried to get her a room in a midtown hotel, but none, it seemed, had vacancies—for a Negro.

The singer, who had been welcomed everywhere she went in Europe, took a room at the Harlem YWCA. She assured Hurok she would be perfectly comfortable in this familiar territory. As usual, Marian Anderson had refused to stoop to battle with the blindly bigoted.

Anderson, who felt that her injured ankle was not "relevant" to her lis-

Anderson, who had finally made up her mind to bring her white accompanist, Kosti Vehanen, back to America, relaxes with the Finnish pianist aboard the Ile de France *in 1935.*

teners, showed up for her concert in a long, black and gold brocade dress that completely covered her cast. Tradition called for a singer to walk onto the stage in view of the audience, but she did not want to make her entrance on crutches.

"To tell the audience I was singing despite a broken ankle would smack of searching for pity," she recalled later, "and I was not there for pity that night. I was there to present myself as an artist and to be judged by that standard only."

Anderson and Vehanen decided to leave the curtains closed until they had taken their places on stage. When the curtains parted, the audience saw the pianist seated and the singer poised in the curve of the piano. Her first selection was Handel's "Begrüssung," an extremely difficult song that begins with a long, sustained note. *New York Times* critic Taubman later wrote, "The very sound of her voice was electrifying. Full, opulent, velvety, it swelled out like a mighty organ."

From that moment on, Anderson had the audience in the palm of her hand. Halfway through, she decided she should explain why she was leaning on the piano, and she briefly mentioned her injury. The response was immediate—and loud. "The house, already adoring, burst into abandoned applause in tribute to her courage," recalled impresario Hurok.

Among those cheering were Anderson's mother and sisters, Giuseppe Boghetti, critics, assorted music lovers, and—quietly sitting in the third row—the ever hopeful Orpheus "King" Fisher. The day after the concert, all the reviews agreed that a new American star had risen. The art of Marian Anderson had finally been recognized in her own country.

Hurok had booked a string of appearances for Anderson and Vehanen, and for the next three months they performed in many U.S. cities, including Chicago and Boston. In March 1936, they returned to Europe to fulfill the commitments they had made there. The highlight of this tour was a concert series in the Soviet Union.

When the train carrying Anderson and Vehanen to Leningrad crossed the Finnish border, it was stopped for inspection by Soviet guards. One of them looked suspiciously at Anderson's portable, windup record player. Vehanen told him what it was and said that the case next to it contained records. Why, asked the guard, were they bringing such things into the country?

Vehanen patiently explained that Anderson was a singer, that she was going to perform in Russia, and that the records were of her voice. Not at all reassured, the guard ordered the train delayed and told the musicians to follow him to headquarters. There he and his colleagues put one of the records on the turntable; the room suddenly filled with Anderson's poignant rendition of "Sometimes I Feel Like a Motherless Child." But how, asked the persistent guard, could they be sure that the voice belonged to the lady in front of them?

Anderson began to sing the same song. Claiming they were still not sure, the guards demanded further vocal evidence, which the singer obligingly provided. As Vehanen noted wryly in his memoirs, "They accordingly had a free recital while trying to convince

Trailed by adoring fans, boxer Joe Louis strides through Harlem in 1935. One critic compared Anderson with Louis, who would win the world's heavyweight championship in 1937.

themselves that what we said was true. Upsetting the train schedule made no difference to them. Apparently good music meant more than having a train leave on time."

Before the tour, Soviet officials had told Anderson not to sing any sacred songs; under communist dictator Joseph Stalin's regime, religion was virtually outlawed in the Soviet Union.

The singer had raised no argument, but in her program were Schubert's "Ave Maria" and several spirituals.

The Leningrad concert, Anderson's first in the Soviet Union, set the pattern for the rest of her appearances there. The hall was packed to overflowing with eager and curious Russians. Before the performance, a Russian interpreter went on stage to announce the song titles and to explain the meaning of their English, German, French, and Italian words. When the interpreter came to "Ave Maria," she called it "an aria by Schubert." She identified the spirituals as "American Negro songs" but said nothing about their religious significance.

The Russians listened to Anderson in absolute silence, but then they applauded and cheered as she finished and left the stage with Vehanen. By the time the performers reached their dressing room, the sounds coming from the hall had changed. Now a roar filled the air; "It sounded," recalled Anderson, "as if the building were being torn up by its roots." The two musicians were listening in bewilderment when the interpreter rushed up and asked them to return to the stage at once. "We did," reported Anderson, "and what we saw astonished us."

The entire audience, including those who had sat in the rear balconies of the cavernous hall, had formed a dense mass in the front of the theater; those closest to the stage were pounding on it with their fists, and others were stamping rhythmically on the floor. Adding to the din were thousands of voices, roaring, "Deep River!" "Heav'n, Heav'n!" "Ave Maria!" Surrounded by adoring Russians, Anderson and Vehanen delivered the encores. "It was disconcerting for a few moments," she recalled, "but how could one resist such enthusiasm?"

Anderson was greeted by similar displays in other Soviet cities. One night

The Kremlin, seat of the Soviet government, was among the sights that greeted Anderson when she arrived in Moscow in 1936. Russians responded to the American singer with wild enthusiasm.

in Moscow, however, the pattern changed. Instead of being brightly illuminated as usual, the theater was dark except for a single, blinding spotlight aimed at the stage. The audience seemed tense and restrained. Red curtains concealed the huge center box from which, in prerevolutionary days, the czar of Russia had watched the stage.

Vehanen asked the stage manager if he would be kind enough to change the lighting, which made reading the music difficult. Looking frightened, the manager said he could change nothing. After the concert, the pianist asked theater officials about the closed box. Had it been occupied? Once again, he confronted fearful faces and silence. He and Anderson later learned the identity of the mysterious listener in the curtained box: It had been the Soviet Union's ironfisted dictator, Joseph Stalin himself.

Moscow was also the scene of a meeting between Anderson and theatrical director Konstantin Stanislavsky, founder of the celebrated Moscow Art Theater. Stanislavsky, who was also famed as the creator of the innovative "method" system of acting, had long admired Anderson's voice. He asked her if she was interested in opera, and she said she was. In that case, said the distinguished Russian, why not stay in Moscow and study the role of Carmen in Bizet's opera?

Soviet dictator Joseph Stalin listened to Anderson's 1936 Moscow concert from behind closed curtains. Although no one saw him, his presence had a chilling effect on the entire theater.

Anderson was, in her own words, "touched and thrilled by the offer." She had, however, committed herself to a long list of engagements. Furthermore, as she later noted, "I was young, and time stretched invitingly before me. What was the hurry? I would return when there was more time."

As it turned out, there was no more time. The Russian director died about a year later, before Anderson had been

Anderson confers with theatrical pioneer Konstantin Stanislavsky. The great director invited her to stay in Moscow and study opera with him, but her busy concert schedule forced her to decline.

able to arrange a return trip to the Soviet Union. "I lost an invaluable opportunity, and I have so regretted it," she said in her autobiography. "It would have been wise to grasp that opportunity even at the expense of postponing the tour."

Anderson's Soviet tour was a spectacular success, but some people criticized her for giving concerts in a communist country. These verbal attacks bothered the gentle singer not at all. "I sang in Russia for the same reason I have always sung anywhere else—to make music," she said. "After all," she added, "it proved that one of my people could be raised up freely in the United States to do the work the Lord had given him the gift to do."

For the next few years, Anderson and Vehanen shuttled back and forth between America and Europe; in 1938 they also made a tour of South America. The ship taking them from Spain to Brazil made a stopover at Dakar, capital of French West Africa (now Senegal).

"Marian seemed happy as her feet

touched African soil," wrote Vehanen in his memoirs. The local women, he reported, stared with great curiosity at Anderson, "their sister who was smartly dressed in European style." She, in turn, was intrigued by the African women, "elegantly adorned in shining robes of many colors, with artistic coiffures."

Spending a day sightseeing, the two musicians happened on a large crowd of people encircling a group of drummers and dancers. "This fascinating and unique performance," said Vehanen, was not staged for tourists, but for

The women of Dakar, reported Kosti Vehanen, were as intrigued with Marian Anderson's appearance as she was with theirs. The singer and her accompanist visited French West Africa in 1938.

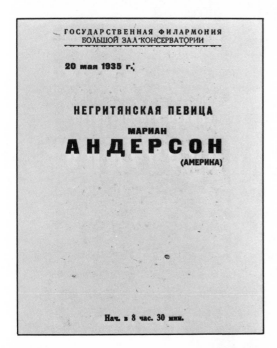

ГОСУДАРСТВЕННАЯ ФИЛАРМОНИЯ
БОЛЬШОЙ ЗАЛ КОНСЕРВАТОРИИ

20 мая 1935 г.

НЕГРИТЯНСКАЯ ПЕВИЦА

МАРИАН

АНДЕРСОН

(АМЕРИКА)

Нач. в 8 час. 30 мин.

Marian Anderson's name, spelled in Cyrillic (Russian) letters, appears on the program for her Moscow concert. The singer quietly ignored Soviet orders to avoid religious music in her programs.

the residents' own pleasure. Neither dancers nor onlookers seemed to mind the presence of the two visitors, who watched with rapt attention as the local people expressed their admiration by "throwing their hats, shawls, and shoes to the dancers."

It was "easy to imagine that we were deep in the African jungle, taking part in a strange performance steeped in old African culture," said Vehanen. "I think for [Anderson] it was like coming home actually to be in the land where her forefathers had lived."

Eleanor Roosevelt awards Anderson with the NAACP's Spingarn Medal in 1939. Calling Anderson one of the era's "greatest singers," Roosevelt also cited her "magnificent dignity as a human being."

Back in the United States, the same "Marian fever" that had swept across Europe was taking hold. As Anderson put it with typical understatement, "My work was drawing the attention of larger circles of people in wider areas of our country." Indeed, impresario Hurok discovered that his hardest job was not finding concert opportunities for his client, but deciding which offers to reject.

Recognition was coming not only from concert audiences, but from the nation's highest officials and most prestigious organizations. In 1936 Anderson had been invited by President and Mrs. Franklin D. Roosevelt to sing at the White House, becoming the first black singer to perform there.

In 1938 Howard University in Washington, D.C., awarded her an honorary doctorate in music. In later years, this artist, who had been refused admission to a small music school in Philadelphia, would receive other honorary degrees from dozens of American universities.

Another honor came in January 1939, when Anderson was named the recipient of the Spingarn Medal. This trophy was awarded annually by the NAACP for "the highest or noblest achievement by an American Negro." The medal was presented to Anderson by first lady Eleanor Roosevelt in July 1939.

During the ceremony, Roosevelt spoke of Anderson's "magnificent dignity as a human being." Calling her "one of the greatest singers of our time," Roosevelt said that "her unassuming manner, which has not been changed by her phenomenal success, has added to the esteem not only of Marian Anderson as an individual, but of the race to which she belongs."

Ironically, between the January announcement of Anderson's Spingarn award and its July presentation, her basic rights as an American were publicly threatened. In April a storm began to swirl about her that would embarrass the entire nation and challenge the concept of democracy itself.

Anderson had always responded to racists with quiet dignity, refusing to be drawn into battle. In 1939, however, she became the center of a furious controversy about black rights.

FIVE

The DAR Controversy

It would be fooling myself," Marian Anderson once wrote, "to think that I was meant to be a fearless fighter; I was not, just as I was not meant to be a soprano instead of a contralto." Nevertheless, in the spring of 1939, Anderson found herself in the middle of a raging battle.

Although racial bigotry has by no means disappeared from the United States, in the years before World War II, it was even more overt and widespread than it is today. Anderson had often seen bigotry's ugly face as she criss-crossed the country on concert tours.

She saw it when hotel clerks took one look at her and suddenly announced a lack of space—even when reservations had been made and confirmed. She felt it, as she once remarked, "in the cold breeze that blew from the persons who were waiting on

me" in restaurants that did not ordinarily serve "colored." She heard it when hotel managers, having grudgingly registered her, suggested that she take her meals in her room instead of in the hotel restaurant. She heard it when strangers addressed her white companions as "Miss" or "Mr." and called her "Marian."

In one southern city, the local concert manager tried to cancel Anderson's recital when she discovered that the singer often took the hand of her white accompanist during her end-of-performance bow. "We won't stand for that here," said the manager. Backed by more enlightened local residents, Anderson sang anyway, taking Vehanen's hand at the conclusion of the concert as usual—but she never returned to that city.

Then there were the countless train rides during which conductors, horrified to discover that a black woman had paid for and was occupying a drawing-room compartment, had protected other passengers from the awful sight by insisting that her compartment door be kept firmly shut.

Early in Anderson's career as a concert performer, she often sang in segregated halls and theaters, although she was never happy about it. She finally refused to sing in any theater that had, as she put it, "an invisible line marking the Negro section from the white." She lost a number of otherwise good engagements because of her position, but she stuck to it.

Most of the fans in southern cities who came backstage to see her were blacks. In her autobiography, Anderson wryly recalled an exception, a white woman who came backstage but who stood apart from the rest of the crowd. When everyone else had left, she handed her program to Anderson. "Since I'm back here," she said, "I'll take an autograph." As Anderson was signing the program, the woman said, "I still don't understand why you didn't sing [the humorous popular song] 'Chattanooga Choo Choo.'" Anderson kept right on writing.

Some people might have thought

Jascha Heifetz (left) clowns with fellow violinist Efrem Zimbalist in the 1920s. In a very different mood in 1939, Heifetz denounced the DAR's contemptuous treatment of Marian Anderson.

that the singer's patience in the face of slights, insults, and outright hostility indicated a lack of courage. But anyone who suspected her of cowardice simply did not know her. A gentle woman who detested confrontations, she saw herself as an emissary, someone who might show racists that they were mistaken. "My mission," she wrote, "is to leave behind me the kind of impression that will make it easier for those who follow."

In her autobiography, she said she tried to show racists that "their attitudes were not based on knowledge." Perhaps, she said, "if they discover that they are wrong about an individual they will begin to realize that their judgment of a group is equally fallacious [mistaken]."

One very hot summer night in Jackson, Mississippi, Anderson sang for an audience of 4,000 enthusiastic people. At the end of the program, she performed several encores, including her customary sign-off, "Ave Maria," but the audience remained in place, begging for more. She obliged with the old American song, "Carry Me Back to Ol' Virginny," which she asked the audience to join her in singing. The crowd raised its voice with, as Anderson described it, "wonderful eagerness and unanimity."

But not everyone was pleased. Several people complained loudly about the "audacity" of a black woman asking whites to join her in song. This time,

however, the racists were in a minority. The following day, the Jackson newspaper published an editorial praising both the singer and her audience. "Sometimes," said the paper, "the human soul rises above itself, above racial prejudices." One of the biggest tests for that "human soul," however, was yet to come.

Sol Hurok, said Anderson in her autobiography, "sought appearances for me in all the places where the best performers were expected and taken for granted." In 1938 Hurok decided the time had come for a recital in the nation's capital. Early in her career, Anderson had sung in schools and churches in Washington, but she had never given a major concert there. There was only one place suitable for such an event: Constitution Hall, the city's largest and most prestigious auditorium.

Constitution Hall was owned by the Daughters of the American Revolution (DAR), a patriotic society formed in 1890. DAR members, of whom there were many thousands, were required to have ancestors who served in the Revolutionary War. They were also required to be white.

In June 1938, Hurok wrote to the manager of Constitution Hall, asking that a date well in the future—April 9, 1939—be reserved for a concert by Marian Anderson. The reply came quickly: April 9 was already booked. Hurok then asked for any of several other dates, but the answer was the same; unfortunately, said the manager, the hall had *no* open dates.

There was obviously more here than met the eye. Hurok asked the celebrated Polish pianist, Ignacy Paderewski, to apply for the same dates. Mr. Paderewski, said the Constitution Hall management, was welcome on any of these days. Hurok's suspicions were confirmed by the chairman of the Howard University concert program. The hall, said this official, had a clause in its rental policy that prohibited "the presentation of Negro artists."

Outraged, Hurok informed the press about the situation. The story, which made front-page news nationwide, shocked Americans. The most dramatic response came from first lady Eleanor Roosevelt, who protested Anderson's exclusion from Constitution Hall by publicly announcing her resignation from the DAR. Other notable members of the organization followed suit, and Americans of all races and from all walks of life raised their voices in support of Anderson.

The renowned violinist Jascha Heifetz, who had already committed himself to a February concert in the DAR auditorium, said, "I am ashamed to play at Constitution Hall." Conductor Leopold Stokowski joined opera stars Lawrence Tibbett, Kirsten Flagstad, and Geraldine Farrar in signing a telegram to the DAR; its ban on Anderson, they said, was "undemocratic and un-

American." *Time* magazine ran an article headlined "Jim Crow Concert Hall," and New York City Mayor Fiorello H. La Guardia sent the DAR a wire saying, "No hall is too good for Marian Anderson."

Some people, of course, took the side of the DAR. Westbrook Pegler, a widely syndicated, ultraconservative newspaper columnist, sneeringly suggested that the affair was a "publicity stunt" staged by a "hitherto obscure Negro singer." And the Washington, D.C., Board of Education turned down Hurok's request to stage an Anderson concert at the city's Central High School.

The school board's rejection set off a new wave of protest. Angry Anderson supporters formed the Marian Anderson Citizens Committee, which picketed the board's offices and gathered 6,000 signatures on a statement denouncing its action. Students at all-white Central High wrote an editorial for their school newspaper, calling for a reversal of the board's decision. They wanted, they said, "the honor of playing host to one of the musical world's greatest artists," and to "prove to the rest of the world that this country holds no grudges because of race or color." The protests failed to move the school board.

What were Marian Anderson's personal feelings? "I was saddened and ashamed," she said in her autobiography. "I was sorry for the people who had precipitated the affair. . . . They

Conservative columnist Westbrook Pegler called Anderson an "obscure Negro singer," although by 1939, she had been applauded at the White House, at Carnegie Hall, and in Europe.

were not persecuting me personally or as a representative of my people so much as they were doing something that was neither sensible nor good."

Reporters from all over the world besieged Anderson with questions: "What is your attitude about the DAR?" "Do you feel insulted by this refusal?" "What do you intend to do about it?"

"I did not want to talk," she said later, "and I particularly did not want to say anything about the DAR." She knew that many DAR members disagreed with the organization's official policy, and she held fast to her conviction "that a whole group should not

Interior Secretary Harold Ickes greets Marian Anderson before her 1939 concert at Washington, D.C.'s Lincoln Memorial. Thousands of people attended the concert; millions more heard it on radio.

Joined by 75,000 Americans, Marian Anderson (left foreground) delivers an exultant rendition of "The Star-Spangled Banner" on Easter Sunday, 1939, in Washington, D.C.

be condemned because an individual or section of the group does a thing that is not right."

The situation was resolved by action from an unlikely quarter: the United States government. On February 24, Secretary of the Interior Harold Ickes— probably at the instigation of Eleanor and Franklin Roosevelt—made Marian Anderson an unusual offer. He invited her to give a free public recital, open to all, on the steps of the Lincoln Me-morial. The concert would be held on Easter Sunday, April 9, 1939.

At first, Anderson was hesitant about the plan. She felt unsuited for "hand-to-hand combat," she hated "a lot of show," and she was unsure about the outcome of such a gesture. "I studied my conscience," she wrote. "As I thought further, I could see that my significance as an individual was small in this affair. I had become, whether I liked it or not, a symbol, representing my people."

Anderson talked it over with her mother. "You know what your aspirations are," said Anna Anderson. "I think you should make your own decision." Her mother, wrote the singer later, "knew what the decision would be. I could not run away from this situation. If I had anything to offer, I would have to do so now."

The concert was scheduled for five P.M. Early in the afternoon a crowd began to gather, and by concert time, a sea of humanity stretched from the Lincoln Memorial to the Washington Monument. A squad of motorcycle policemen escorted Anderson and Vehanen to the platform that had been built in front of the memorial.

Despite her years of experience, despite the innumerable concerts she had given, despite the fact that she had been called one of the century's greatest singers by Arturo Toscanini, Anderson was terrified. "My heart leaped wildly, and I could not talk," she said in her autobiography. "I even wondered whether I would be able to sing."

Mustering all her professionalism, she displayed an outward calm. "The arm which I took to steady her," recalled Sol Hurok, "was steadier than my own." She was introduced to the dignitaries who had assembled for the concert, although, as she said later, "If I did not consult contemporary reports I could not recall who was there." Present were Supreme Court justices, sen-

Young admirers, hoping for a closer view of Marian Anderson, strain at police ropes after the singer's triumphant 1939 Easter concert in Washington, D.C.

ators, congressmen, diplomats, cabinet members, and other high government officials.

Introducing Anderson, Interior Secretary Harold Ickes noted that the monument to Abraham Lincoln was a fitting place for this concert. "Today," he said, "we stand reverently and humbly at the base of this memorial to the Great Emancipator while glorious tribute is rendered his memory by a daughter of the race from which he struck the chains of slavery."

Concluding his speech, Ickes said, "Genius, like justice, is blind. . . . Genius draws no color line. She has endowed Marian Anderson with such a voice as lifts any individual above his fellows, as is a matter of exultant pride to any race."

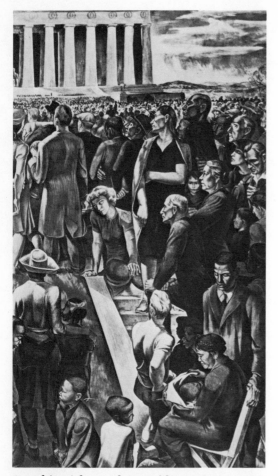

A multiracial crowd assembles at the Lincoln Memorial in artist Mitchell Jamieson's view of Anderson's 1939 concert. Unveiled in 1943, the mural is still on exhibit at the Interior Department.

Anderson stepped out from the memorial's towering marble columns and looked at the expectant faces of 75,000 men, women, and children of all races. "I had a feeling that a great wave of good will poured out from these people, almost engulfing me," she wrote later. She began to sing "The Star-Spangled Banner," her voice soaring over and blending in with the voices of the multitude before her.

Anderson's program included "America," the aria "O Mio Fernando," Schubert's "Ave Maria," and several spirituals. When she finished, a roar from the crowd exploded the stillness of the Washington evening. "I am overwhelmed," she said. "I can't tell you what you have done for me today. I thank you from the bottom of my heart again and again."

At that point thousands of people rushed toward the stage, reaching out their hands to Anderson. Walter White, secretary of the NAACP, later recalled a little black girl in the surging crowd. She was dressed in her best clothes for Easter, and her face was streaming with tears. White said, "If Marian Anderson could do it, the girl's eyes seemed to say, then I can, too." The nation had joined, as historian William Manchester put it, "to give prewar America's civil rights record one shining moment of glory."

Not long after the Easter Sunday concert, the Department of the Interior commissioned a mural commemorating the event. Anderson was invited to Washington for its 1943 unveiling. At the ceremony, Secretary Ickes called Anderson "a symbol of the willing acceptance of the immortal truth that [in the words of Abraham Lincoln] 'all men are created equal.'"

Responding to the tribute, Anderson

A Texas bus passenger points to a segregation notice, outdated after the U.S. Supreme Court banned segregated transportation in 1956. Anderson had patiently sought such goals for decades.

said, "I am deeply touched that I can be in any way a symbol of democracy. Everyone [at the concert] was a living witness to the ideals of freedom for which President Lincoln died. When I sang that day, I was singing to the entire nation."

Anderson had accepted an invitation to sing at a benefit concert after the unveiling. The invitation had come from the DAR, and the concert was held at Constitution Hall.

Characteristically, the singer took no personal credit for the end of segregation at the Washington auditorium. "When I finally walked into Constitution Hall and sang from its stage, I had no feeling different to what I have in other halls," she said. "There was no sense of triumph." Noting that "the hall is now open to other performers of my group," she did admit, however, that "there is no longer an issue, and that is good."

Interviewed by eager reporters in London, Anderson tries to avoid questions about the painful DAR controversy. "Could I have erased the bitterness," she said, "I would have done so gladly."

SIX

The Mature Artist

Marian Anderson had been famous long before the historic Washington concert on Easter Day, 1939, but after it, she was a superstar. Letters and calls requesting her appearances poured into the Hurok office. Many of the invitations, of course, had to be turned down, but there was one that could not be refused. It was from the White House.

King George VI and Queen Elizabeth of England were scheduled to visit President Franklin Roosevelt and his wife, Eleanor, in June 1939. To entertain their royal guests, the Roosevelts invited an all-star roster of American singers. They included Lawrence Tibbett of the Metropolitan Opera, radio personality Kate Smith, cowboy singer Alan Lomax, and contralto Marian Anderson. After the show, the entertainers would be presented to the king and queen.

About to meet the leaders of the two most powerful nations in the world, all the performers, including Anderson, were nervous. Before she met the president, she prepared what she called "a little speech suitable for such an occasion." Roosevelt was known for his charm and easy manner, but he was nevertheless an imposing figure. As soon as she was introduced, Anderson said later, "My pretty speech flew right out of my head." She barely managed to mumble, "Good evening, Mr. President."

Resolving to do better with the British monarchs, Anderson went off to do some private practicing. "I had seen people curtsy in the movies," she recalled, "and it looked like the simplest thing in the world." Faced with the queen of England, however, she found it not quite so simple.

"I was looking into the queen's eyes

Meeting in Washington, D.C., in June 1939 are (left to right): Britain's King George VI; President Franklin D. Roosevelt and his military secretary; Eleanor Roosevelt; and Queen Elizabeth.

when I started my curtsy," she said later, but she somehow wound up with her back to the queen. Always ready to enjoy a laugh at her own expense, she added, "I don't know how I managed it so inelegantly, but I never tried one again, not even for the king!"

Despite Anderson's problems with royal protocol, the glittering White House audience warmly applauded her performance, which included "Ave Maria" and the spiritual, "My Soul Is Anchored in the Lord." Anderson was especially pleased by the enthusiasm of Eleanor Roosevelt, whom she admired enormously.

Anderson and Roosevelt's paths often crossed after the White House

gala. It was Eleanor Roosevelt who presented Anderson with the Spingarn Medal the following month, and the two met again at a benefit concert a year later. In her autobiography, Anderson recalled a meeting with the first lady in Japan, where the singer was making a concert tour.

Surprised to run into Anderson in a Tokyo hotel lobby, Roosevelt asked what she was doing there. Anderson explained that she was giving a series of recitals. "When are you singing in Tokyo?" asked Roosevelt. "Tonight," replied Anderson.

"I knew from my own experience with the Japanese that an extensive program would be arranged for her," wrote Anderson. "I hate to think how her hosts had to rearrange their plans for her that evening, but she was at the concert. . . . I shall never forget that she took the time to come and listen." Anderson, who called Eleanor Roosevelt "one of the most admirable human beings I have ever met," also said, "I suspect that she has done a great deal for people that has never been divulged publicly." Remembering the Easter Sunday concert in Washington, Anderson added, "I know what she did for me."

In her autobiography, the singer described an occasion when she expressed her admiration for the first lady in a somewhat unconventional way. As she was leaving a theater where she had performed one evening, the stage manager told her that Eleanor Roosevelt would be lecturing there the next day and would be occupying the same dressing room. "And so," wrote the dignified singer, "on the large mirror I left a greeting, written with soap."

Anderson and Vehanen made 92 concert appearances in the 1939–1940 season. After that, the Finnish pianist decided it was time to return to his native land. The two good friends parted, and Anderson acquired a new accompanist. He was Franz Rupp, a highly gifted German pianist who had fled his country when Adolf Hitler's Nazi party assumed power there.

Smiling in the snow after a concert in the early 1940s are (left to right): impresario Sol Hurok; Franz Rupp, Anderson's new accompanist; Anderson; and road manager Isaac Jofe.

Rupp, who would remain as Anderson's accompanist until she retired 25 years later, was an expert on German lieder. Especially well versed in the songs of Schubert, he offered her a new perspective on this repertoire. As well as being a superb accompanist, Rupp served Anderson as manager of sightseeing expeditions, locater of rehearsal studios, and, in emergencies, piano tuner. He was, said Anderson, a "jolly" traveling companion and "really good company."

The third member of the Anderson team was Isaac Jofe of the Hurok office. Jofe, who acted as Anderson's road manager, was responsible for planning bookings, accommodations, and transportation. This was a big job; during the years that Jofe worked with Anderson, she traveled some hundreds of

Franz Rupp and Marian Anderson plan the program for an upcoming concert. Rupp, a refugee from Nazi Germany who became Anderson's accompanist in 1940, remained with the singer for 25 years.

Sharing a triumphant moment with her mother, Marian Anderson displays her latest award, the Philadelphia Medal, in 1941. The singer was the first black to receive the prestigious trophy.

thousands of miles by train, car, ship, and plane, most of them scheduled by Jofe.

And it was Jofe's responsibility to smooth out any difficulties created by local racism. Even after the national display of support for Anderson during the DAR incident, racial discrimination was very much alive in the United States. The most difficult problem remained the booking of hotels, many of which were still reluctant or even unwilling to accept a black guest—even if she was Marian Anderson.

The Hurok agency's policy, carried out by the determined Jofe, was to tell local concert managers that decent hotel accommodations near the concert hall were necessary. If they could not be arranged, Jofe would explain, there would not only be no Anderson concert, there would be no other Hurok artists booked into that city. Although Anderson still sometimes stayed in private homes on tour, this policy proved generally effective.

Anderson, Rupp, and Jofe, who spent more time with each other than with anyone else, came to think of themselves as a family. The two men got along well together, but they often had different opinions, particularly about the selection of songs for each concert. Jofe, recalled Anderson, usually favored selections that were "melodic, surefire," whereas Rupp would campaign for compositions that showed "musical originality."

Traveling together between appearances, the trio engaged in what Anderson called "extended powwows," reviewing and criticizing each performance. The singer enjoyed these sessions, but she noted that her male companions "relish arguments more than I do." Not limited to music, their conversational subjects ranged from politics to economics to literature. The men, said Anderson, were "both lively and sharp-witted—Franz Rupp, who describes himself as a 'Yankee mit accent,' and Jofe, with his hearty interest in all aspects of life."

Now that she was a major artist, Anderson received high fees for her performances. After she had established her relatives on firm financial ground, she began to extend her generosity beyond the family. She started by donating the proceeds from a 1940 Carnegie Hall concert to four of her favorite organizations: the NAACP, the National Urban League, the YMCA National Council, and the International Committee on African Affairs. In 1941 she got an even better chance to aid others.

The Philadelphia Award had been presented to the city's outstanding citizen every year since 1921. Established by Edward Bok, the crusading editor of *The Ladies' Home Journal* from 1889 to 1919, the award brought not only great prestige, but a cash prize of $10,000, a huge sum in 1941. Anderson had long been aware of the Philadelphia Award but, as she said in her autobiography, "It never occurred to me that I might one day be a recipient."

Notified that she *was* the recipient for 1941, Anderson was both surprised and honored. The prize had been awarded only once before to a woman, and never before to a black person. When the time for the presentation came, the singer felt her usual nervousness about being in the spotlight for anything but a concert. "I don't recall what I said," she wrote later, "but I do remember that I ended in song, with the words of the spiritual: 'I open my mouth to the Lord, and I will never turn back.' "

Anderson had received—and would continue to receive—many awards,

Anderson (right) congratulates soprano Camilla Williams, two-time winner of the Marian Anderson Award. Anderson had established the scholarship prize with her own award money in 1941.

but she was especially pleased by this one because, she said, "It led to something in which I take special pride." She used the prize money to set up a scholarship program for aspiring vocalists of all races. "I remembered from my own youth," she said, "that many young singers need help to go on with their studies." Over the years, Anderson's program has aided dozens of young singers, including the now renowned sopranos Grace Bumbry and Mattiwilda Dobbs.

After the United States entered World War II in 1941, many artists donated their talents to the nation's war effort. Anderson gave free concerts at military bases and hospitals and performed at war-bond rallies.

Visiting a women's army camp in Des Moines, Iowa, in 1942, Rupp and Anderson form an impromptu choir with a group of officers. The pair often toured military bases during World War II.

With celebrated black American baritone Paul Robeson, Anderson sang and sold bonds at Lewisohn Stadium, the site of her 1926 recital with the New York Philharmonic. In 1944 she broke the record for war-bond rallies by raising $1.7 million at a Carnegie Hall concert.

The singer thoroughly enjoyed performing for servicemen, whom she called "a wonderful audience." Because most of the men in uniform were young, and many had limited educations, Anderson was advised to limit her military concerts to simple music. She was happy to discover that the restriction was not necessary. "One did not have to sing down to these men," she wrote. "One could sing the things one sang regularly, and they seemed to be delighted."

She found the same thing true of defense workers. At one point, she was invited to come to a California shipyard to christen a new warship, the *Booker T. Washington*, named for the famous 19th-century black educator. As she began to sing for the dignitaries attending the christening ceremony, she became aware that all around her—on the decks of unfinished ships, perched on scaffolds, and high in the ships' riggings—were shipyard workers, listening intently to each note. When she finished, the yard rang with cheers and loud demands for encores. So much, she thought, for "singing down" to average citizens!

The war years, during which Anderson both pursued her singing career and fulfilled a crowded schedule of public-service appearances, allowed her little private life. For one very important personal activity, however, she had no difficulty in finding time.

King Fisher, now a prominent architect, had been appearing, disappearing, and reappearing in Marian Anderson's life for 20 years. He had never given up hope of persuading her to marry him, and at last, in 1943, she said yes. The wedding took place in a small Connecticut church that July.

Deciding they wanted a home in the country, the newlyweds began looking at property in New Jersey, Long Island, and Connecticut. They saw several places they liked, but these properties were not, as Anderson discreetly put it in her autobiography, "available to us." What she meant was that she and Fisher were once again facing an old, vicious problem. In many of the affluent suburban areas, blacks were not welcome.

Ironically, Fisher had very light skin and was often mistaken for a white. Once he had even tried "passing" as white in order to further his career in the then all-white field of architecture, but had soon found the pretense repugnant. Like his wife, he was proud of his race. And, also like his wife, he believed he had the right to live anywhere he could afford to live. "Even if you want to indulge in some luxury for the good of your soul," Anderson had once written, "why should not one [race] have the privilege as well as the other?"

The Fishers eventually bought exactly what they had been looking for, a rambling old farmhouse situated among meadows and woods near Danbury, Connecticut. King Fisher immediately named the new place Marianna Farm.

Here the architect, described by his wife as "one of the handiest men I have ever seen," designed and built a separate studio where she could practice undisturbed. He also dammed up a small brook to make a swimming pool and did much of the house remodeling himself. Marianna Farm, which be-

A California shipyard worker, impressed by Anderson's vocal performance during christening ceremonies for the warship Booker T. Washington, *gives the singer an appreciative handshake.*

came the Fishers' permanent residence, served as a haven for Anderson after long, exhausting concert tours, and, eventually, as a perfect spot for her retirement.

Anderson had been a long time deciding whether or not to marry Fisher, but once she took the step, she knew it had been the right one. She rarely made public statements about her personal life, but when a reporter asked her about her new status as a wife, her response was from the heart. "Marriage to King," she said, "was worth waiting for." In her autobiography, she wrote, "King and I have had some lovely times together." She called him

Marian Anderson leaves a concert hall with Orpheus (King) Fisher, the longtime suitor whom she finally married in 1943. She told a reporter that "marriage to King was worth waiting for."

Cuddling a family pet, Anderson relaxes at her Connecticut estate, Marianna Farm. The singer and her husband bought the property soon after their long-postponed wedding in 1943.

"an understanding person," whose patience with her frequent absences on tour made it possible for her to maintain both career and home life.

As for her career as a housewife, Anderson was the first to admit to a decided lack of talent. "I try to be a homemaker," she said, but her efforts in the kitchen were almost always disastrous. She enjoyed telling the story of one of her greatest culinary fiascos. On this occasion, the Fishers had invited a guest to dinner on their housekeeper's day off.

Anderson put a beef roast in the oven, then went off to work in her studio. When she took the meat out of the oven, she recalled, "My heart sank. The poor thing was shriveled and hard." Fisher tried to carve it, but it was unyielding. "As for the rest of the meal," said the cook, "the spinach was hot but not very soft, and the potatoes, though they looked good, were hard inside."

"That was not very good, was it?" she said after the meal.

"No, darling," said her husband, "it was not. It was very bad. But you get an E for effort."

"The truth," continued Anderson, "is that the meal was so bad it was funny, and we laughed and laughed." Their guest gallantly said he planned to brag to his grandchildren that "Marian Anderson prepared a whole meal for me."

"Please," begged Anderson, still laughing, "don't tell them what kind of meal!"

The year 1943 also brought Anderson her first decoration from a foreign country. The government of Liberia, an African country founded in the 19th century as a haven for former slaves, awarded her its highest honor, the Liberian Order of African Redemption. The medal was given, said the citation, in recognition of Anderson's efforts to promote international good will.

The singer continued with her concert tours in the 1940s. At the beginning of each season, she and Rupp met

King Gustav VI of Sweden decorates Anderson with his nation's Litteris et Artibus medal in 1952. The award was one of hundreds received by the singer from countries all over the world.

in the studio at Marianna Farm to choose the repertoire for the next series of recitals. Her programs always included the spirituals with which she was so strongly identified, and they usually also featured songs by Schubert, her favorite composer. The composers she liked best after Schubert were Brahms, Bach, and Handel.

Two of the spirituals that Anderson performed most often were "Heav'n, Heav'n" and "Deep River." She often said, however, that her favorite was "He's Got the Whole World in His Hands." This song, she said in her autobiography, "reminds us not to lose sight of the fact that we have our times of extremity and that there is a Being who can help us at such a time.... It is more, much more, than a number on a concert program."

Anderson was showered with honors during the 1940s and 1950s. In 1946 the Women's Division of Jewish Charities named her as a "Key Woman of the Year," and the Finnish government gave her its coveted Order of the White Rose. In 1952 she received the Litteris et Artibus award, given annually to outstanding artists and scientists by the government of Sweden. In that year she was also named a "Woman of Achievement" by the Federation of Jewish Women's Organizations and given the Page One Award by the Philadelphia Newspaper Guild. During the following two years she received honorary degrees from Smith College, Temple University, and Moravian College.

In 1955 Anderson reached another milestone in her long career. Like many of her other achievements, this one would open a very important door for the black American singers of the future.

Anderson and Metropolitan Opera manager Rudolph Bing inspect the auditorium where, on January 7, 1955, she would become the first black to sing with the historic New York City opera company.

SEVEN

To the Metropolitan and Beyond

When Marian Anderson was young, she had dreamed of singing opera. She had confided her hopes to her voice teacher, Giuseppe Boghetti, but he had gently discouraged her. It was not, he said, a field open to black artists. Russian director Konstantin Stanislavsky had offered her a chance to study *Carmen* with him, but she had let the opportunity slip away.

By the time she was 53, Anderson had almost forgotten her early dream. But now she got an offer that would open a new chapter in the history of American music.

In September of 1955, Sol Hurok brought a British production of Shakespeare's *Midsummer Night's Dream* to New York. He celebrated the occasion by giving a huge party for the city's theatrical and musical elite, naturally including Marian Anderson and her husband, King Fisher. Disliking crowded parties, the couple had decided not to go, but as they drove home from the opening of the Shakespeare play, Anderson changed her mind.

She described the ensuing events in her autobiography. "I have a strange feeling that we should go to the party and say hello," she said to her husband. He agreed, turned the car around, and headed for Hurok's apartment.

At the party, Anderson was approached by a tall, distinguished man; he was Rudolf Bing, general manager of the Metropolitan Opera. Not bothering with small talk, Bing got right to the point: "Would you be interested in singing with the Metropolitan?" Not sure he was serious, Anderson just looked at him, and he repeated the question. Finally she said, "I think I would."

Bing said the role he had in mind

Anderson gets a signal from conductor Dimitri Mitropoulos as she rehearses for her Metropolitan Opera debut. She said preparing for her first operatic role made her feel "incredibly alive."

was that of Ulrica, an old sorceress, in Verdi's opera, *The Masked Ball*. The part was short, but it was highly dramatic, requiring both a beautiful voice and a powerful stage personality. The next day Bing sent Anderson a score for the opera.

When she read Ulrica's part, she thought it was too high for her voice, and almost turned it down. But she had promised Bing she would study the role and then sing it for Met conductor Dimitri Mitropoulos, and she believed in keeping promises.

Still unsure that she was suited for the part—"There is a high A in Ulrica's aria," she said later, "and I must confess that I was not too happy about it"—she auditioned for Mitropoulos. When she finished, he told her, "You haven't worked on it enough yet." Anderson said she was willing to study it for another week or two and then try again. The conductor agreed, and she went home. There she got an urgent message: Call Sol Hurok at once.

The impresario greeted her call with one word: "Congratulations!" To her astonishment, Anderson learned that as soon as she left Mitropoulos, he had called Hurok, demanding a contract for her appearance in *The Masked Ball*.

"The excitement was too much," recalled the singer. She telephoned her husband, her mother, and her accompanist. Then she went to work. When she arrived at the Metropolitan Opera House, she was touched by the greeting of a stagehand: "Welcome home," he said.

No black singer had performed with the Metropolitan Opera since its founding in 1883, and Anderson's upcoming appearance made national headlines. A *New York Times* editorial commented on the news: "That Marian Anderson has fulfilled a lifelong ambition is not nearly as important as the fact that we have another opportunity to hear her in still another medium," said the newspaper. "When there has been discrimination against Marian

Anderson," it added, "the suffering was not hers, but ours. It was we who were impoverished."

The next weeks were filled with lessons in acting and Italian, along with rehearsals. Appearing with Anderson would be two famous opera stars, Yugoslavian soprano Zinka Milanov and American tenor Richard Tucker. It was an exhilarating time for Anderson. "Somehow all this caused the blood to rush through me with new meaning," she wrote later. "I felt incredibly alive, able to do any amount of extra tasks."

At last opening night came. The opera house was jammed to the rafters and buzzing with excitement. Particularly expectant were the occupants of the center box—King Fisher, Sol Hurok, and Marian Anderson's mother and sisters. When the curtain rose on the second scene, "sorceress" Marian Anderson was alone on stage. She was dressed in rags, wearing a long black wig, and stirring a huge, smoking kettle.

A wave of applause swept through the theater, and soon the whole audience joined in a standing ovation. Mitropoulos signaled the orchestra for silence until the demonstration was over. "I felt myself tightening into a knot," recalled Anderson. "I had always assured people that I was not nervous about singing, but at that moment I was as nervous as a kitten." Then she began to sing.

Her hand resting on a human skull and her expressive features framed by a long black wig, Marian Anderson makes a formidable Ulrica, the sorceress in Verdi's opera The Masked Ball.

Music critics in the audience were aware of her initial uneasiness. "At first she wavered a little, no doubt under the special tensions of the occasion,"

The Masked Ball *cast takes an opening-night curtain call. Left to right are opera stars Richard Tucker, Roberta Peters, Zinka Milanov, Marian Anderson, and Leonard Warren.*

said one. By the end of her aria, however, Anderson had won their hearts. "The climax of the scene," wrote critic Olin Downes, "was sung with such meaning that she stamped herself forever in the memory of all who listened."

When the opera was over, the cheering audience demanded one curtain call after another. Metropolitan Opera policy forbade solo bows, but the shouts of "Anderson! Anderson! Anderson!" continued until the singer, after getting what she called "a little push" from her fellow performers,

walked out on stage alone. Her reappearance was greeted by a barrage of applause.

Backstage after the performance, reported Anderson, the always efficient Isaac Jofe "acted like a combined receptionist and traffic cop" as crowds swirled toward her dressing room. Finally, she was alone with her mother. Anna Anderson threw her arms around her daughter and whispered, "We thank the Lord."

"Though she is not outwardly demonstrative," said the singer, "I could see that there was a light around

Anderson's Metropolitan Opera appearance paved the way for a host of other black singers, including (left to right): Robert McFerrin, Gloria Davy, Grace Bumbry, and Leontyne Price.

The Sea of Galilee forms a backdrop for the domes and towers of Tiberias, an ancient city in northern Israel. Anderson was deeply moved by her 1955 visit to the new Jewish nation.

her face. She did not know much about opera, but she knew the significance of what was going on that night and she was profoundly moved by it. If she had said more, she would have said, My cup runneth over.'"

Anderson, who called her experience with the opera company a "high-light" of her life, said that she felt "privileged to serve as a symbol." She took pride, she said, in knowing that her appearance as Ulrica had encouraged other black singers "to realize that the doors everywhere may open increasingly to those who have prepared themselves well."

Doors did open. After Anderson's historic performance, other black singers—including Robert McFerrin, Gloria Davy, Mattiwilda Dobbs, Martina Arroyo, George Shirley, Grace Bumbry, and Leontyne Price—have appeared with the Metropolitan Opera. As Howard Taubman of the *New York Times* put it, "Miss Anderson—like Joshua, but more quietly—had fought the battle of Jericho and at last the walls had come tumbling down."

When the Metropolitan season ended, Anderson and Franz Rupp took off for another concert tour, this time to Israel, North Africa, France, and Spain. Both the singer and her accompanist were especially eager to visit Israel, which Anderson's Jewish grandfather had often talked about, and where Franz Rupp's brothers and sister lived.

They were not disappointed. In Israel, where Anderson "found the spirit of a new tradition in the making," she also discovered audiences who were "something special." She and Rupp were enthusiastically received by his family at the *kibbutz* (communal farm) where they lived.

The two musicians arrived at the start of Passover, one of Judaism's most joyful holidays, and they were invited to a huge, traditional *seder*, the special Passover feast. Here, noted Anderson, "Some thousand people joined in a common celebration. The seder and the gathering were impressive and moving." She was also struck by the "emphasis this kibbutz put on music." Deciding "that there was a great deal of potential talent" among the local musicians, Anderson reacted characteristically: She set up a scholarship fund for young Israeli singers.

Anderson wanted to see everything in this exciting land. She visited Jerusalem, the Mount of Olives, and the Dead Sea. She also made a point of seeing the Jordan River, that waterway

Franz Rupp and Marian Anderson share a light moment during a concert rehearsal in the 1950s. An impeccable professional team, the two were also devoted offstage friends.

Visiting Seoul, South Korea, during her State Department-sponsored tour of the Far East in 1957, Anderson accepts an honorary degree from Ewha Women's University.

pressed his emotions and dreams in terms that were closest to him—terms from the Bible." She said she "could see in Israel the geographic places that represented the reality [of religion], and they stirred me deeply. I kept thinking that my people had captured the essence of that reality and had gone beyond it to express in the spirituals the deepest necessities of their human predicament."

Back home after the long tour, Anderson spent the summer of 1956 relaxing with her husband at Marianna Farm. While she had been abroad, her autobiography, *My Lord, What a Morning*, had been published, earning high praise from book reviewers.

In January 1957 she proudly complied with President Dwight D. Eisenhower's request that she sing "The Star-Spangled Banner" at his second inauguration. Later that year she received five more honorary college degrees; among them were doctorates from Rutgers University and the University of Rochester.

In the years following World War II, both the United States and the Soviet Union were working hard to demonstrate their friendship for the world's underdeveloped nations. As part of that effort, the U.S. State Department asked Anderson to make a goodwill tour of the Far East. This would be a major undertaking: The schedule called for a 35,000-mile trip and visits to 12 foreign countries.

whose name she had so often mentioned in song, as well as the site of the famous walls of Jericho.

Anderson had always been deeply religious; seeing with her own eyes many places she had read about in the Bible was an emotional experience for her. "It came to me," she wrote after visiting Jericho, "that the Negro made images out of the Bible that were as vaulting as his aspirations.... He ex-

Accompanied by Franz Rupp, Anderson set out in the fall of 1957. Their first stop was South Korea, where American troops were still stationed in the aftermath of the 1950–1953 conflict between North and South Korea. At U.S. military bases in Korea, homesick servicemen whistled, stamped, and cheered after each of Anderson's songs. They were especially responsive to "Home Sweet Home," at the end of which she usually gave the soldiers a big wink—a theatrical sign-off that the magazine *Musical America* had called "the best in the business."

Anderson and Rupp next performed in Seoul, South Korea's capital. Here the singer received an honorary degree from Ewha Women's University. "You are respected as a leader among women," said the citation. "Your success against great odds has encouraged others in their struggle for justice and human rights."

After Korea, the stops included Vietnam, Thailand, Taiwan, Burma, Pakistan, and India. Whether she sang in a small church or a huge outdoor stadium, Anderson usually held an informal discussion group after the program. The Asian audiences were surprised and pleased by her friendly and unpretentious manner, and they reacted with obvious delight to her music. Particularly popular were "He's Got the Whole World in His Hands" and "Let My People Go."

Asked thousands of questions about

Burmese premier U Nu and his wife greet Anderson after her 1957 concert in Rangoon. He called her performance "a rare combination of good voice, good technique, and good dramatic acting."

everything from baseball to her personal life, she answered with frankness and good humor. At one stop, a reporter asked her if she would be willing to sing for Orval Faubus, the governor who had illegally sent the state militia to keep black students out of Arkansas schools.

This was a tough question, but Anderson's answer was worthy of a seasoned diplomat. She would, she said serenely, "be very delighted to do it" if Faubus "would be in the frame of mind to accept it for what it is, for what he could get from it."

In India she won many friends when she paid a reverent visit to the me-

Conferring with Anderson about "The Lady From Philadelphia," his TV documentary about her 1957 goodwill tour, journalist Edward R. Murrow traces her route on a globe of the world.

morial for Mohandas Gandhi, the beloved Indian leader who had been assassinated in 1948. Riots almost occurred in New Delhi, the Indian capital, as eager thousands struggled to see her. A story filed by a *New York Times* correspondent said, "The big thing to do in New Delhi today was to find someone with enough pull to get you into the Marian Anderson concert."

Well-known broadcast journalist Ed-

ward R. Murrow traveled with Anderson and Rupp, recording the tour for a film documentary. Entitled *The Lady From Philadelphia*, Murrow's film was shown on his popular television program, "See It Now," in late 1957.

The Anderson documentary, which *Newsweek* magazine called "probably the most widely applauded show in TV history," was admired by viewers across the country, even in the deep

South. The State Department, aware that Anderson's presence had scored points for the United States among millions of citizens of the Third World, arranged for the film to be shown in 79 foreign countries.

The diplomatic skills that Anderson had displayed on her triumphant tour were approvingly noted by the president of the United States, already one of her admirers. Citing Anderson's "deep sense of humility" and "firm belief in the universal brotherhood of man," in 1958 Eisenhower named her a member of the United States delegation to the United Nations.

The president's choice was widely praised. The *New York Times* said Anderson's appointment "may be construed as a recognition of her own unique worth. We like to think, however, that it is rather a way in which the United States does honor to the world organization."

Delegate Anderson, who took on her new assignment in the fall of 1958, became a member of the important UN Trusteeship Council. This group was responsible for overseeing the administration of countries that were changing their status from colonies to independent, self-governing nations. Anderson's particular responsibilities were the newly liberated African nations of Togo and Cameroon.

Anderson felt that she could make a contribution to her country by increasing its sensitivity to Third World nations. She said she could understand, perhaps better than some of her fellow delegates, "a great many things that motivated the hopes and pleas and demands of the little nations, particularly those whose people are dark-skinned."

Her colleagues agreed emphatically. She was, said the U.S. delegation's chief delegate, Henry Cabot Lodge, a "most effective member," one who was "extremely well liked and respected by all." Other delegates concurred, calling Anderson "diligent," "articulate," and a person who "did her homework well."

At the end of her one-year term at the UN, Anderson returned to her concert tours, collecting even more honorary degrees as she went. Princeton and Northwestern universities were among the eight institutions that awarded doctorates to her during the next two years.

When the nation's new president, John F. Kennedy, was inaugurated in 1961, he followed the example of Dwight Eisenhower by inviting Marian Anderson to sing the national anthem. She and the young chief executive liked each other at once. The following November, Anderson conferred with Kennedy and West German Chancellor Konrad Adenauer about the work of the Freedom from Hunger Foundation, an organization she had helped to create. The foundation's goal, as its name implies, was the eradication of famine throughout the world. Anderson also

President John F. Kennedy (second from right) introduces Anderson to West German chancellor Konrad Adenauer (right) at the White House in 1961. Next to Anderson is politician George McGovern.

enjoyed a number of sparkling visits to the White House, both as a performer and as a guest, during the three years of Kennedy's presidency.

In December 1963, she sang for him again, but this time things were very different. The occasion was a memorial service following Kennedy's assassination on November 22. Reporting on the somber service, the *New York Times* said, "Marian Anderson, her eyes closed, her voice echoing through the plaza and reechoing beyond the skyscrapers, sang three Negro spirituals, 'Let Us Break Bread Together,' 'Hear De Lam's a-Crying,' and 'Ride On, King Jesus.' There was none of the spirit she demonstrated when she sang at President Kennedy's inauguration. The crowd . . . did not applaud—but it was not easy."

A few days later, Anderson received the Presidential Medal of Freedom from Lyndon Johnson, Kennedy's successor. Her nomination for the prize had been made by her friend, John F. Kennedy. When he presented the medal, Johnson said, "Marian Anderson, artist and citizen . . . has ennobled her race and her country, while her voice has enthralled the world."

Anderson's receipt of the Medal of Freedom was applauded by her countless fans, none of them prouder than her mother. Anna Anderson had watched with quiet joy as her daughter rose from obscurity to world renown. She had witnessed that daughter's courage and determination over and over again. She had sympathized during times of trouble and rejoiced at her successes. And she had given her daughter the strong religious faith that allowed her to cope with adversity.

On January 10, 1964, soon after Marian Anderson received her nation's highest civilian honor, Anna Anderson died at the age of 89. Her daughter later said she was glad her mother had "lived long enough to realize her three girls appreciated the sacrifices she'd made for them"—sacrifices that had helped make possible Marian Anderson's extraordinary career.

By 1964 that career had spanned more than four decades and won Anderson the admiration and respect of millions of people throughout the world. She had come far, breaking new ground for her race and establishing new standards for her art. Now, she decided, it was time to let the next generation of singers add to the foundation she had built.

Hand in hand, Marian Anderson and Franz Rupp acknowledge the cheers of their Carnegie Hall audience. Anderson's retirement in 1965 produced an outpouring of "bravos," applause — and tears.

EIGHT

"The Voice of the American Soul"

She stepped across the stage and the applause rose from the audience in a sweeping, throbbing wave. Her eyes glistening, her lips in a tight smile, she whispered, 'Thank you, thank you.'

"Suddenly, dramatically, the entire audience—2,900 persons—stood, clapping, cheering, and acclaiming the woman on stage—Marian Anderson."

These words were part of a *New York Times* report on the final concert of Anderson's career, held in Carnegie Hall on Easter Day, April 19, 1965. The performance climaxed a tour that the singer had begun the previous October in Washington, D.C.'s Constitution Hall.

As the thunderous applause continued on this Easter Sunday, Anderson, who had just completed her fourth encore, was urged to sing one more song. "No," she said slowly. "It's finished."

Then she turned to her husband. "Now," she said with a smile, "I'm going to be a homemaker."

Unlike the instrument of a violinist or a pianist, the instrument of a singer—like that of an athlete—ages along with its user. There comes a point when a vocalist's body can no longer generate the immense energy required to produce clear, sustained tones. Anderson had been considering retirement for several years, but each time she had mentioned the subject to friends and advisers, they had persuaded her to sing for another season. Finally, at the age of 62, she had taken the decisive step.

"To say farewell to Marian Anderson will not be easy for the American people," wrote correspondent Vincent Sheean. "Rain or shine, war or peace, she has been before us now for 30 years as a living part of the national consciousness, the voice of the American soul."

Even after Anderson's official retirement, she remained at the center of America's artistic life, and she continued to be showered with honors and awards. At the invitation of the French government, she revisited the West African nation of Senegal, where she took part in the 1965 Festival of Negro Arts. In 1966 President Lyndon Johnson appointed her to the National Council on the Arts, a group that reviewed grant applications from American artists. Two years later the National Associa-

Composer Aaron Copland conducts a performance of his "Lincoln Portrait," the dramatic orchestral piece in which Marian Anderson starred in 1976.

tion of Negro Musicians presented her with its first Humanitarian Award. In 1973 she was elected to the National Women's Hall of Fame.

During America's bicentennial year, 1976, Anderson went on the road again, this time as an actress. Touring in composer Aaron Copland's *A Lincoln Portrait*, a work for narrator and orchestra, she appeared with major orchestras across the nation. Thousands of Americans—many of them young people who had never heard her before— thrilled to the sound of her deep and beautiful voice reading the words of Abraham Lincoln.

When Anderson turned 75 in 1977, her admirers organized a huge birthday party at Carnegie Hall, where she was feted by many of the nation's foremost musicians. Among them were violinist Pinchas Zukerman, conductor James Levine, and opera singers Leontyne Price, Shirley Verrett, and Clamma Dale.

Price, a black soprano who had become one of the nation's top operatic stars, had followed Anderson's footsteps at the Metropolitan. After an emotional speech at the party, she summed up her indebtedness to her predecessor in six eloquent words: "Simply because of you, I am." Other birthday tributes included the United Nations Peace Prize, the New York City Handel Medallion, and a congressional gold medal, presented by first lady Rosalynn Carter.

Soon after the party, King Fisher suffered a major stroke. With Anderson constantly at his side, he worked hard on the exercises his doctors ordered, but the stroke had permanently damaged his ability to speak. Although most people now found it difficult to understand him, Anderson had no trouble communicating with her "young man" (as she always referred to him). The couple remained as close as ever for the rest of King Fisher's life. Afflicted by a series of further strokes during the next few years, he died in 1986.

In December 1978 the John F. Kennedy Center for the Performing Arts in Washington, D.C., presented its first annual awards for "lifetime achievements in the arts." Honored by the center in an elaborate ceremony were dancer Fred Astaire, choreographer George Balanchine, composer Richard Rodgers, pianist Artur Rubinstein— and contralto Marian Anderson.

The tribute to Anderson began with singer Harry Belafonte's introduction of a film about her life; next came Anderson's favorite spiritual, "He's Got the Whole World in His Hands," sung by Aretha Franklin and the Howard University Choir. Anderson then made a typically modest speech in which she spoke of her lifelong trust in God. "When things happen along the way which might pull one up rather sharply, through disappointment," she said, "think on your faith and go back,

Observing Marian Anderson's 75th birthday in 1977, first lady Rosalynn Carter (right) prepares to present the beaming singer with a special gold medal awarded her by Congress.

Marian Anderson will be remembered not only for her glorious voice, but for her dignity, her quiet courage, and her insistence on the right of all Americans to pursue their dreams.

Opera stars Shirley Verrett (left) and Grace Bumbry flank Marian Anderson on her 80th birthday, which was celebrated with a gala party at New York City's Carnegie Hall in 1982.

so to speak, to the well to be replenished."

After her retirement, Anderson spent as much time as she could at Marianna Farm, but the honors continued to roll in, and she made a point of personally accepting as many as she could. In 1979 she returned to Philadelphia, which had proclaimed August 22 as "Marian Anderson Day."

The day's celebrants included popular operatic tenor Luciano Pavarotti, whose benefit concert raised $100,000 for the establishment of the Marian Anderson Library and Scholarship Fund at the University of Pennsylvania. The singer, who had donated her papers to

the university, responded to the tumultuous applause of her fellow Philadelphians by saying simply, "This is one of the greatest moments of my life."

Anderson's place as one of America's greatest artists is secure. But she will be remembered for much more than her magnificent voice. Speaking at the singer's 80th birthday celebration, black opera star Shirley Verrett called her a "dreammaker." Anderson, said Verrett, had given those who came after her "the right to dream the undreamable, reach for the unreachable, and achieve the impossible." Verrett said Anderson's courage "changed the course of history" and "cast a shadow that embraces us all."

Anderson had not set out to change history. She had wanted only the right to work hard and to develop the talent she believed God had given her to share with mankind. But in the course of her quiet, determined progress toward that goal, she expanded horizons for Americans of all races.

Maintaining a serene faith that "a way would be found" to overcome difficulties, she refused to be goaded into what she saw as unproductive confrontations. Her religious belief—and her belief in herself—gave her the strength to endure racist indignities that contemporary readers may find hard to believe.

While there is still racial injustice in the United States today, the ugly rac-

King Fisher and his wife, Marian Anderson, relax from a horseback ride at Marianna Farm. After 43 years of happy marriage, Fisher suffered a fatal stroke in 1986.

Anderson receives an honorary doctorate from the University of Connecticut in June 1987. University officials said Anderson "allowed us, in doing honor to her, to do a great honor to ourselves."

ism that afflicted the nation during Anderson's youth has diminished. Part of the credit for that belongs to Anderson herself. She said she was not "designed for hand-to-hand combat," but she never backed down on her quiet insistence that America owed equal rights to all its citizens. At the same time, she never preached hatred, violence, or separatism. She was convinced that it was essential to have "an understanding of your fellow men, even though in some instances they behave so poorly."

An interviewer once asked her what she thought about laws that mandated school integration and fair housing and employment practices. Did Anderson believe that racial equality would be achieved by such legislation? "Not by those laws alone, as wonderful as they are," she replied. "They've certainly widened the path and carried it way ahead. But you have to accomplish the little things too."

Anderson went on to plead for "understanding," which she had always seen as the key to racial harmony. "The Negro or the white person," she said, "must be judged as an individual, with all his goodness or badness, and the color of his skin makes no difference. He who made us all did not make any mistake when he made us of a different color."

Because Anderson detested what she called "showing off," much of the help she gave others was known only to a small circle of people. She was extremely generous—with her time, with her talent, and with her money. Never forgetting that the kindness of fellow church members had enabled her to begin her musical career, she often aided young singers and other artists by giving benefit performances, making direct contributions, and establishing scholarship programs.

After her retirement, she allied herself with a vast array of charitable causes. The long list of associations she aided includes American Freedom from Hunger, the Spence-Chapin Adoption Service, the Play School Association, the Eleanor Roosevelt Foundation, and the American National Red Cross.

Innumerable words of praise have been spoken about this remarkable woman. Perhaps her friend Sol Hurok best summed up her legacy. "In any century," said the impresario, "only a handful of extraordinary men and women are known to countless millions around the globe as great artists *and* great persons. Only a few inspire the adoration and respect of the mighty and humble alike. In our time there is Marian Anderson."

FURTHER READING

Anderson, Marian. *My Lord, What a Morning.* New York, Viking, 1956.

Hurok, S., and Ruth Goode. *Impresario: A Memoir.* New York: Random House, 1946.

McNeer, May, and Lynd Ward. *Give Me Freedom.* New York: Abingdon Press, 1964.

Newman, Shirlee P. *Marian Anderson: Lady from Philadelphia.* Philadelphia: Westminster Press, 1966.

Peavy, Linda, and Ursula Smith. *Dreams into Deeds.* New York: Scribners, 1985.

Sheean, Vincent. *Between the Thunder and the Sun.* New York: Random House, 1943.

Sims, Janet L. *Marian Anderson: An Annotated Bibliography and Discography.* Westport, CT: Greenwood Press, 1981.

Southern, Eileen. *The Music of Black Americans: A History.* New York: Norton, 1971.

Truman, Margaret. *Women of Courage.* New York: Morrow, 1976.

Vehanen, Kosti. *Marian Anderson: A Portrait.* New York: McGraw-Hill, 1941.

CHRONOLOGY

Feb. 17, 1902	Marian Anderson born in Philadelphia, Pennsylvania
1908–22	Sings with Union Baptist Church choirs
1916	Meets black concert singer Roland Hayes at a church concert
1918	Studies voice under Mary Patterson
1919	Begins voice lessons with prominent vocal coach Giuseppe Boghetti
1920	Embarks on first concert tour, performing at churches and schools throughout the South
1922	Meets Orpheus Fisher (future husband)
1923	Wins first prize in Philadelphia Philharmonic Society vocal contest
1924	Gives Town Hall recital in New York City
1925	Wins National Music League competition
	Gives concert with New York Philharmonic Orchestra
1931	Studies in Berlin on Rosenwald scholarship
1932	Performs in Norway, Sweden, and Finland
1933	Embarks on successful two-year concert tour of Europe
1935	Signs with concert manager Sol Hurok
1936	Performs in the Soviet Union
	Becomes the first black singer to perform at the White House
April 9, 1939	Gives Lincoln Memorial concert after being barred from Constitution Hall by the Daughters of the American Revolution
1941	Establishes scholarship award for young singers
1943	Marries Orpheus Fisher
1955	Becomes the first black to sing with New York City's Metropolitan Opera Company
1956	Publishes autobiography, *My Lord, What a Morning*
1957	Sings at inauguration of President Dwight Eisenhower
	Makes U.S. State Department-sponsored tour of the Far East
1958	Serves as U.S. delegate to the United Nations
1961	Sings at inauguration of President John Kennedy
1963	Receives the Presidential Medal of Freedom
1965	Retires after giving farewell concert at Carnegie Hall
1976	Narrates Aaron Copland's "A Lincoln Portrait" in a nationwide tour
1978	Receives Kennedy Center award for lifetime achievement in the arts
1982	Celebrates 80th birthday at Carnegie Hall

INDEX

PICTURE CREDITS

Tony Bacewicz/The *Hartford Courant:* p. 104;   The Bettmann Archive: pp. 12, 15 (left), 16, 23, 26 (top), 27, 28, 38, 42, 46, 47, 60 (top), 64, 75 (bottom), 86, 90, 100;   Culver Pictures Inc.: pp. 18, 77, 101 (bottom);   Lisa Larsen/*Life* Magazine: p. 103;   Metropolitan Opera Archives: pp. 60, 87, 88, 89 (top left), 89 (top right), 89 (bottom left), 89 (bottom right), 93, 94, 98;   The New York Public Library: pp. 17, 22, 24, 26 (top right), 26 (bottom right), 32, 34, 35, 36, 37 (top), 37 (bottom), 45, 48, 62, 70, 75 (top), 78, 79, 81, 92;   Scurlock Studio: p. 68;   Springer/Bettmann Film Archive: p. 49;   UPI/Bettmann Newsphotos: pp. 29, 55, 56, 57, 67 (top), 69, 71, 72, 74, 96, 101 (top), 102;   Van Der Zee: p. 15;   Van Pelt Library/University of Pennsylvania: pp. 11, 14, 20, 30, 39, 40, 44, 50, 52, 53, 58, 59 (bottom), 67 (bottom), 76, 80, 82, 84, 91

Anne Tedards, a professional singer, holds a master's degree in Vocal Performance from the University of North Carolina at Chapel Hill. Her articles have appeared in various periodicals of the music industry.

❖   ❖   ❖

Matina S. Horner is president of Radcliffe College and associate professor of psychology and social relations at Harvard University. She is best known for her studies of women's motivation, achievement, and personality development. Dr. Horner serves on several national boards and advisory councils, including those of the National Science Foundation, Time Inc., and the Women's Research and Education Institute. She earned her B. A. from Bryn Mawr College and Ph.D. from the University of Michigan, and holds honorary degrees from many colleges and universities, including Mount Holyoke, Smith, Tufts, and the University of Pennsylvania.